RENAISSANCE LOST

For Lee

Because you taught me how to fall

PROLOGUE

A cloud of blood and dust exploded before my eyes in the parking lot of a dingy nightclub outside of Dallas, Texas, on a humid summer night. I was twenty years old.

I fell onto my hands and knees. Blood dripped from my head onto the pavement in front of me. Somewhere beyond the blood, probably three inches from my head, I heard a blast. Mortality laced with pistol smoke. They had my full attention now. I was abandoned by my best friend and, more importantly, by my own rationale. I forgave him and accepted my fate. Pain and suffering had become a way of life. I scarcely made out a cluster of words through the deafening silence of gunfire.

"Where the fuck is DaVinci? He owes me three million dollars," said the voice within the dust.

DaVinci, my missing mentor. DaVinci, the man who disappeared from a hotel in Las Vegas and left me with a million dollars in a duffle bag.

"I brought you the money from Las Vegas!" I yelled.

I looked over at Mike, still lying in a pool of blood. Groans of anguish escaped from his mouth.

"You're two million dollars short."

They gave me no opportunity to respond.

"Kill him. Do it quick—"

"—Wait! I have DaVinci's clientele in Philadelphia. I'll get the money."

There was a long silence. The dust began to clear. Relieved, I tried to stand but was held in place.

"You have one shot."

Bullets dumped out and scattered across the pavement. One round slid back into the chamber. My future spun in the cylinder, then snapped back into the frame.

"One shot will determine your fate."

A finite choice loaded in the pistol was laid on my left shoulder.

Mike awoke from the haze of his own dark fate and reached toward me, "Don't—

His voice was light years away.

I thought of everything I loved in this world.

I took the gun and put it to my head.

I thought of Vinny, I thought of Sammy, and I thought of Lana. At that moment, an unexpected and terrifying thought burned through my consciousness.

Who am I?

I pulled the trigger.

SPRING

1.

Life began for me in Philadelphia, Pennsylvania, in 1984. My father was a gunslinger, and my mother was a nurse. They were married, and they loved each other, at least for a time.

My father was a brilliant, hard-working military man, but he was no father. Due to his military service, we often moved from place to place, and he was absent from the family for extended periods. He never spoke about his work, but I think the emotional scars from what he was trained to do left him in constant conflict with himself. To deal with his demons, my dad moved to New York City, drank late at night in the bars in Manhattan, and was a gun-toting wild man high on cocaine.

As an adult, I learned more about the true nature of my dad's job after he was discharged from the military. He did private contract work in other countries, mainly the Philippines. I remember seeing photos of him holding a gun while escorting the president of the Philippines in the early 1990s.

As a small boy, I remember he loved to sing *Dead Man's Party* while throwing me in the air as we danced together. I was always terrified he would drop me, but he never did. He gave me that record along with my very own record player on my seventh birthday.

My mother was a natural beauty with a strong work ethic and a commanding personality, but she was no mother. My mom attended nursing school when she was young and had three sons, including me. School and work consumed her time, allowing her only a few windows of opportunity to see us. Frustrated, lonely, and overworked, she looked for a way out.

As an adult, I would learn that my mom wrote a letter to my dad demanding that he take custody of my brothers and me, or we would be claimed as adjudicated dependents and placed in a foster home.

As a small boy, I remember she loved to watch *Journey to the Center of the Earth* while running her fingertips through my hair until I fell asleep on her lap. The only gift I can recall from her was a card on my twelfth birthday that read:

I miss my son.

Their love for each other only extended so far. He drank copious amounts of alcohol, smoked profusely, and subsequently got into heated arguments with my mom. On more than one occasion, my dad burned me with a cigarette as I attempted to break up their fights.

"Please promise me you will quit smoking," I said.

"I love you, and I promise I will," he said as he tucked me into bed and recited his favorite proverbs from the Torah.

"Hope for a miracle, but don't rely on it... If things aren't as you wish, change them... be wise in deeds, not words... learn by failure... pride with an abundance of virtues chokes them all... endure the bad... pain is human... *Gam zu l'tova.*"

To this day, I can feel the stubble of his beard against my face, scratching my cheek when he kissed me goodnight.

After their divorce my dad moved to Fort Dix, New Jersey. Between his secretive job and drug addiction, my dad was non-existent for the majority of my adolescence. Father and Son's Day at school for me was always an embarrassment. I gave my mom an ashtray I had made for him in school, hoping she would give it to him on Father's Day. She looked at it, then looked at me.

"Your father is like a cigarette. He stinks, he's toxic, and he always burns me if I let him get too close."

In 2012, several phone calls were made from the Philippines to my brother regarding my dad's health. Soon after, I learned that he died of heart failure from drugs, alcohol, and smoking. However, the coroner's report indicated that his body had sustained severe physical damage when he was found dead. The type of injuries he sustained indicated that he died by other means, but no one truly knows what happened.

I'm the youngest of three brothers. All of us were born within a year apart. Sammy is the oldest brother and, for most of my life, has served as a father figure to me. His unique charisma can only be described as a shit-talker who gets away with it because he's good-looking. He has an iconic nature about him, a demeanor reminiscent of James Dean and Edward Norton.

Vinny is my middle brother, mentor, and voice of reason for me, particularly in times of turmoil. He is level-headed and taught me to use my humor to de-escalate conflicts. He gave me the courage to use my mind instead of my fists. Despite each brother's different roles in my life, they shared one philosophy in common.

"A man leads by action. His word is his bond, and if being a gentleman doesn't work, just punch 'em in the fucking mouth."

Vinny had a twin, my brother Jonathan, who died shortly after birth. As a result, my parents decided to have another child, and that is how I came to be in this world. My first few moments alive were of near death, as I was born being strangled by the umbilical cord around my neck. Sometimes, I feel like I'm living in someone else's shoes or, perhaps, living on borrowed time. I've always wondered which son my mom meant in that birthday card.

***

I was seven years old when my mom remarried a man named Greg. Charming, old school, and funny. He knew how to captivate a room. He could make you think a stranger was his best friend. Raised during the iron fist era of discipline, Greg was the type of guy who was perpetually past his treatment date for his blood pressure medication. My mom adored his stature and easy smile but perhaps confused his roughness for strength.

My earliest memory of him was when my mom put him in charge of watching us while she worked the night shift to make ends meet. The night was quiet except for a baseball game on the television. I sat at the table in the kitchen reading my favorite comic book *The Amazing Spider-Man* as Sammy sat across from me.

"I want some," I whined.

Each time I tried to get my spoon in the ice cream Sammy shifted the carton in the opposite direction.

From the living room, Greg heard us arguing and leaned up in his recliner.

Sammy was eating mint chocolate chip ice cream directly from the carton. Anyone who has seen *Seinfeld* knows it's not kosher to double-dip. Sammy ignored him.

Greg exploded into the kitchen and grabbed Sammy by his shirt. I jumped between them. Greg's fury turned to me. His fists knocked my head side to side. I collapsed on top of the ice cream carton. When Greg stopped I got up and ran for my life.

For the rest of the night, I hid under the bed. I peed myself because I was too scared to leave my room and use the bathroom. What I remember most wasn't the pain, it was the fucked up contradiction between hot and cold.

I awoke in the morning, cracked the door, and looked for Greg before I scrambled to the bathroom. The edge of the sink dug into my hips while I sipped water from the faucet. When I dropped down I examined myself in the mirror. Both ears and the area around my temples were purple and swollen.

That day at school, I was questioned by my teachers about the bruises. I told them the story that my mom had prepped me with before leaving for the bus that morning. I explained that the injury had occurred while wrestling with my brother, but the looks on their faces said they weren't buying it. Still, I stuck to the lie.

When I arrived home from school, my mom and Greg sat me down and told me how much they loved me. I approached them like you would a tiger at the zoo.

"I love you very much," she said. "Greg loves you too."

I raised my head and looked at her.

"It's important that you know we love you." She squeezed his hand. "Greg could be in serious trouble if anyone finds out what happened. He could go to *jail*."

I only realized the gravity of the situation when she used the term jail. I felt bad that I'd caused such a problem. I nodded that I understood. They appeared to be relieved. This was the first time they manipulated my love, which led to a lifetime of confusion about the definition of the word. How could love be so brutal?

When I was ten years old, I was sent to a new school called Assumption B.V.M. I tried my best to fit in but being a Jewish kid in a Catholic school I knew deep down inside that I didn't belong there.

"How is it that you never got into using drugs like both of your brothers?" Greg would ask me years later.

"Simple... I was never an altar boy," I said.

The whole religion-based school curriculum wasn't for me. One day, I landed in trouble for not singing in church, as was required of every child. I was honest when I was questioned about my lack of enthusiasm.

"I'm Jewish. I don't want to sing."

The nuns looked at me as if I had just killed Jesus and put him on the cross myself.

The following day, I was headed out the front door for school when the phone rang. A nun had taken it upon herself to call my house to inform my parents that I hadn't been singing in church. Greg picked up the phone. I paused with the door open and watched him from the living room. He hung up the phone, charged at me, and slammed the door shut. I was trapped. He whipped my legs repeatedly with a thick leather belt. Each crack punctuated his words.

"You'll! Sing! In! Church! You! Hear! Me! Sing! In! That! God damn Church!"

When Greg was finished, he opened the door and shoved me outside. I froze, not from the snowy Philadelphia weather but from the shock of what happened. My clothes were ripped all over. My body throbbed in pain. I tried to compose myself as I stood waiting at the bus stop.

Finally, the school bus arrived. Embarrassed, I boarded the bus and walked to the rear in an attempt to hide, but I couldn't sit down because of the stinging pain in my legs.

"Sit down!" the bus driver yelled.

"I can't!" I yelled back.

As we drove to school, I stood while the other kids whispered and stared at me. My legs pulsed with pain. If I sat down, I wasn't sure if I'd be able to stand up again. Panic washed over me as the bus got closer to school.

The driver must have reported me to the school officials because my teacher confronted me about my behavior when I arrived. I was instructed to wait in the hall to be escorted to the principal's office.

It was in that hall that I first realized a brother could be someone outside of my immediate family. Mike was a kid I had noticed before but had never spoken to. I only knew who he was because he had a unique platinum blonde hair color. He was returning from the principal's office when he stopped and spoke to me.

"Are you in trouble, too?" he asked.

"Not exactly," I replied.

"Well, what is it then?"

I said nothing. Mike saw the look on my face and noticed my ripped clothing. He extended his hand to me. I shook it.

"You'll be ok. My parents suck, too."

I don't know how he knew... but he knew. I felt relief and camaraderie with a stranger through that simple act of kindness. Mike would eventually become my first partner in crime. I trusted him with my life.

The teacher exited the classroom to escort me to the principal's office, but not before scolding Mike for talking to me.

"Back to class, Mr. Santoro!"

Mike ignored the teacher. He looked back at me.

"See you on the other side."

The principal pointed to a chair when I walked into the office and gestured for me to take a seat. I was forced to decline the offer. They told me I was safe and gave me some snacks to help calm me down.

Eventually, I trusted them enough to admit that Greg had whipped me with a belt. I was escorted to the nurse's office so they could gather evidence and document the abuse. Standing in front of three women, I don't know what was worse, the beating or the shame I felt when I was asked to remove my pants. They gasped when they saw the bruises. My legs were dark purple from my ankles up to my buttocks.

The school officials held me late into the evening, well past the end of the school day. I was grateful and relieved that my teachers had rescued me from my family. Now that the truth about my parents was out in the open, I would be safe. What happened in the following hours would lay the foundation for a lifetime of mistrust in authority figures.

2.

My first taste of road rash came when I was sixteen years old. My skin was burned a deep cherry red from my upper thigh to just below my lower ribs.

I did not discriminate against career opportunities. If money knocked, I answered the door. My job was to make this Honda CBR 1000RR disappear for the owner, who had fallen into debt over the sky-high monthly payment plan. The motorcycle was worth around thirty thousand dollars, brand new. When stolen, about ten thousand.

The night was cloudy, with the forecast calling for light rain. It was the perfect cover for a little bit of breaking, entering, and liberating. Before I entered the garage, I cut my escape hole in the fence for a hasty getaway.

The keyhole was in shambles. The ignition didn't want to cooperate with me, and I'll admit it, I was rough. I jumped in the saddle, backed up the bike, and pushed it into the neighborhood behind me to figure out the problem with the ignition.

The steering column would lock if I slowed the motorcycle to below five miles per hour. I worked on the bike under a dull orange street light, rain pouring down, head to toe in black, with a ski mask on in a wealthy suburban neighborhood. Fuck me— *here comes a hero*. I heard a scream from a nearby house.

"Stop! I'm calling the police!"

I pushed the bike as fast as I could, hopped on, popped it into first gear, and felt it roar to life. I had to be double on the clock now.

I emerged from the shadows and headed toward Mike, who sat parked nearby, waiting to trail behind me as we escaped. I revved the motorcycle until it screamed, sending a signal to Mike to let him know I was coming. He pulled out and trailed behind me in a stolen Corvette to keep up with me in the event of a high-speed chase.

The rain whipped and stung my eyes like mace. I opted for a ski mask as my only protection because I hated how helmets reduced my field of vision. The odometer pushed one hundred miles per hour. Fear was riding on the back seat of the motorcycle with me. As I let go and pushed harder, fear flew off the bike and tumbled into the night. In fifth gear I hit one hundred thirty. I found myself on the verge of leaving this world and entering another.

The road ahead was straight for another two miles. The voice of reason in my head said no, but the bike said yes. I flicked my wrist a quarter of an inch and accelerated to a hundred forty miles per hour. Death rode beside me in the darkness. Fear was long gone.

I roared past two police cars parked semi-hidden behind a nearby building. Based on how fast I was going, I wasn't sure whether or not they were going to take chase. For a moment, it was quiet. I saw nothing. I turned the corner and saw them start to pull out. Still, no lights flashed as they followed me from afar. The seconds became longer... one... two... three... four.

Sirens cut through the night as red and blue light painted the buildings behind me.

Good show, old boys.

I wanted to go faster, but the bike couldn't handle the wet road, especially around the turns, which allowed the police to gain on me. Mike did his best to keep up, pacing between myself and the cops. He was now in a second-hand chase himself, attempting to save me. Blinding rain caused me to come into the turn too late. A short marriage between tire and asphalt was instantly divorced. The motorcycle disappeared from underneath me.

An invisible hand tore me from the handlebars. Launched in the air, torn between sky and ground. My body was tossed like laundry in a dryer. I had no concept of up or down. Split seconds of the moon, half-obscured by clouds. I came to a rest stretched out on the pavement. Mike came skidding to a halt alongside me and threw the passenger door open.

"Get the fuck in!"

I peeled myself up off the wet concrete and jumped in. Police cars were coming from every direction. We sped towards a crowded intersection. This chase was just getting started, or so I thought.

Bang!

It sounded like a bomb went off behind me. It was the sound of my head bouncing off the window as we spun through the intersection. Our car struck a barrier, bounced back, and rolled across three lanes of traffic.

White powder exploded from the airbags and burned my eyes. When the car finally came to a stop, only one thought came to me.

Run.

The overpass was fifty yards away. What lay beneath it was unknown. The cops were breathing down my neck. My chest ignited and combusted. I ran until my lungs pumped fire. Sirens split my ears, as police lights nagged me. I felt the long arm of the law reaching out for me as I arrived at the edge of the overpass. I climbed over the wall, looked down, and jumped into the night.

I held my breath as I fell through the darkness.

Lady Luck caught me in her safety net. There was almost no impact as I fell into a steep grassy incline and slid down to a muddy ditch. Mike tumbled down the hill, flipped, and landed hard near the bottom.

Bleeding profusely, and holding his ribs, he needed medical attention. Silhouettes in emergency lights stood above us on the overpass. I picked him up, pulled Mike's arm over my shoulder, and ran in the opposite direction from the police and paramedics.

3.

All the other students had long since gone home. I sat alone in a classroom, awaiting my fate. I was expecting the police to arrive with some social workers. Perhaps I was heading to a foster home.

Moments later, the principal and teachers walked into the room and told me I would be going home. The room began to spin. There would be no rescue or intervention. No one was coming to save me.

Only years after this incident did I piece together why the church had decided to send me home. Money and reputation were of primary importance to the institution. To be clear, I'm not telling you this to paint myself as a victim. I simply wish to illustrate my lack of understanding of the business of the adult world. I know some children had it far worse than I did. At the end of that school year, several staff members, some of whom were aware of my injuries, were transferred to another parish. I would later learn that there were allegations of child sex abuse at Assumption B.V.M.

Not only was I going home, but I was going to have to face Greg after I turned him into the authorities. They were putting me back into the hands of the same man who, just twelve hours prior, had beaten me so badly that

I couldn't sit down.

My mom picked me up from school. The ride home was painfully silent. It was quiet at the house that night until Greg came home. I was standing in the kitchen next to my mom when he lunged at me and grabbed me by the throat.

"You fucking rat!" he screamed as he threw me to the floor. He kicked me repeatedly. I covered my face with my hands.

"You say my fucking name to anyone again, and I'll kill you!"

That evening, I lost faith in every adult figure I had ever known. Despite the fact that I didn't fit into a Catholic school, it had served as a refuge for me before that day. A place outside the oppressive atmosphere of my home. With that refuge gone, I began to harbor resentment toward my parents, teachers, and authority. Slowly but surely, I started to rebel.

***

1997 was the year I saw pink. I was thirteen years old. The day after Thanksgiving, my brother Sammy went out drinking with his friends to celebrate the holiday. The last time I saw our friend Rob alive, he and Sammy were walking down the street carrying two cases of Honey Brown beer, heading out for the night.

The next day, the police came to our home to speak with my parents. All I heard was that Rob was dead, and the rest of them were lucky to be alive. My family was in shock when my brother came home from the hospital with a slew of stitches across his head. I asked him what happened.

"We got hit by a train. Rob's dead. I woke up facedown in a puddle, choking. I don't ever want to talk about it again."

This was the first and last time my brother spoke about the accident.

The following day, my parents told me what happened. Sammy, Rob, and two other friends were walking along the train tracks, drinking at night, when a train came from around the bend. The train appeared to approach them from a parallel set of tracks, but no one ever looked back to confirm which side it was on. They were walking in line one behind the other when they were struck by the train. Rob was the first to be struck. He knocked them off of the train tracks in different directions.

Greg brought me to the site of the accident the next morning. Pink chunks of brains lay on the railroad ties, still covered in blood. I couldn't believe what I saw when I looked up. A single black Vans low-top with a white stripe down the side dangled high above me from a tree branch. It was one of Rob's sneakers. No human could've survived the impact it would've taken to launch a shoe that high into the air.

At the funeral, his mother sobbed loudly over the loss of her son. She was heartbroken. I remembered Rob was a funny guy who spent a lot of time with me and my brothers, but sadly not anymore. His death was a heroic tragedy that saved their lives.

I approached the coffin and said goodbye to Rob. I could see that his body had suffered a tremendous amount of damage. I recognized him, but not as the same person I knew. I had no idea at the time, but this accident would set into motion a series of events that would change the course of my life.

***

My first interaction with law enforcement came later that year. I was picked up for trespassing through a yard that was a well-known shortcut in my neighborhood. The owners were fed up with kids walking through their property and called the cops on me. I was written a citation, and the police called my parents to inform them of the incident.

When I walked in that evening, my parents were waiting for me. My mom screamed and took a swing at me. I blocked her punch and saw Greg getting up out of his chair. His favorite chair. The one that he sat in every night when the Phillies played on TV. He charged at me full throttle. I was standing in the exact spot where he had beaten me so badly three years before on that cold winter day.

I burst out the front door. Greg took chase. A clear sensation of his fist spiked my memory, then my adrenaline. I ran for my life. I attempted to slow him down by running over the hoods of parked cars. He was athletic and hurdled them like a walk in the park. His rapid footsteps crept and grew louder than mine. After only one block he caught up with me at the corner bar. I felt his crushing presence even before he tackled me in the parking lot.

A crowd of drunken patrons poured out of a nearby bar when they heard the commotion. At first, I thought they were going to break up the fight. However, this being Philadelphia, they apparently, had only come outside to cheer me on. I circled the parking lot, but I got outboxed. They watched on as he ruthlessly smashed my head into the edge of the metal dumpster. The impact left an indentation on my forehead that still can be felt to this day.

"Kill me, just fucking kill me!" I screamed.

Finally, Greg backed off. The difference between this attack and the last one was that I knew there would be no repercussions for him. That's why I fought back. After I stood up for myself, Greg never tried to hurt me again.

***

Rob's death was a turning point in our household. Sammy's drinking and drug use reached an all-time high. He never forgave himself for what happened to Rob. He hated our house and decided to run away from home. I followed him for hours and begged him to return. I would've been lost without him. My brothers were the only source of comfort and guidance I had. Sammy eventually came home, but this was part of a pattern of escapism that would continue for years.

One of our family friends owned a local pizzeria called Mama Russo's. They were having a birthday party for one of their sons. We had a blast celebrating with them, eating pizza, wings, and cheesesteaks. When the cake came out, Sammy told me he wanted to go home. I asked him what was wrong, but he refused to tell me anything and walked out before we all sang *Happy Birthday*.

After we finished our cake, I decided to go home and find out why Sammy was acting so weird. When I walked into the house, it was quiet and empty with no lights on. I yelled upstairs for Sammy to come down to play Nintendo. There was no reply. At first, I thought maybe he wasn't home, but I decided to go upstairs and check.

A line of light traced the rectangular frame at the end of the hall. It was the silhouette of a closed door. My gut told me that something was wrong. I knocked on the door.

"Sammy, are you in there?"

I opened the door slowly and found my brother with a rope around his neck tied to the corner post of the bunk bed. His face was dark red from the pressure building up in his head, but he was still breathing. I ran into the room and picked him up the best that I could. Gasping with the rope still tied around his neck, he tried fighting me off. He wanted to die. I bear-hugged him, lifted him with all my might, and refused to let go. Reluctantly, he caved and removed the rope from around his neck. I stared at him in disbelief. I had no idea he was in so much pain.

I remembered something that the priest had said at Rob's funeral: *the Lord giveth and the Lord taketh away*. I couldn't help but wonder when the giveth part would come again.

4.

The first thing I saw was the fog. It hung thick over the train yard as we walked alongside the boxcars. Mike trailed behind me in the twilight. The floodlights in the distance reflected off the tracks that lay between us.

"How much is on the table?" I asked.

"Fifty thousand, give or take," Mike replied.

When he explained what the job entailed, my gut told me it was a bad idea, and that's how I knew it was a good idea. I was sixteen years old, and fifty thousand dollars was a hell of a lot of money. This was only a scouting mission. The real job came two weeks later.

On the evening of the heist, we set out in the cover of the night as a four-man team broken up into two groups. Two guys would board the train and throw off only the most expensive merchandise. Two guys on ATVs would drive alongside to retrieve the goods as we threw them off and later serve as our getaway.

After we surveyed the train yard, we located the specific boxcar that Mike and I needed to board. That was the easy part. My job was to cut the lock, take only the expensive merchandise, and find one crate in particular.

I wore a small oxygen-acetylene torch backpack, tinted goggles, and heavy leather gloves. I turned on the valves and ignited the acetylene with a striker. I began mixing it with oxygen until the tip formed a sharp blue flame. The lock melted away like butter.

We climbed into the boxcar and waited. It felt like an earthquake as the train started to move. A slow rumble gradually became louder as the momentum increased. Trees became blurry. The train was moving much faster than I had anticipated. A frightening thought struck me.

How the fuck am I getting off this thing? Am I going to end up like Rob?

I guess Mike didn't think this part through. Fuck it.

We started chucking crates out the door to clear a path between us and our target. The ATVs began to follow a breadcrumb trail of high-valued items. Halfway through the tightly packed crates, we found the specific one that we had come for. I broke the lock and opened it. I was in awe as the flashlight illuminated the contents of the crate. It looked like a lost treasure. *Pulp Fiction* came to my mind.

"We happy? Vincent... we happy?"

"Yeah, we happy."

We secured the designated cargo inside large duffle bags and heaved them out the door into the cavern of night. Time wasn't on our side, and we needed to get off the train before we hit the next yard. This play was over, and it was time to exit stage left.

I stepped up to the threshold of the boxcar and looked down. The ground rushed by me in a blur. In no way, shape, or form was I excited about taking a leap of faith off this steel monster. We looked for a safe place to jump, but the train was moving too fast, and we couldn't see anything in the darkness. Mike looked at the ground, then back at me, and yelled over the roar of the train, "On the count of three, we jump."

I laughed at him.

"What are we, *Thelma and Louise*? Punch yourself in the stomach, let your balls drop, and fucking jump!"

The ground hit with such a force that it knocked the wind out of me. I rolled for what felt like hours in a wave of grass, rocks, and fallen tree branches. My body was tossed around like a rag doll in a dog's mouth. The luck of the human coin toss was on my side. I landed on tails, but Mike didn't fare as well. He landed on heads and slammed into something that tore a quarter-sized hole in his arm.

Mike was tough as nails. The first thing that he said to me when I helped him to his feet was, "No hospitals."

Blood poured out from his wound as I tried to wrap it up. Mike didn't complain, but why me, why was I blessed? We both knew the risk you take when you ride the gravy train is that when you walk out the door, it might be your last time.

5.

Late one evening in 1998, Greg packed up his stuff and left our house for good. I was fourteen years old.

"He divorced me because of you boys," my mom said.

She cried in my arms. I hugged her, held her close, and told her, "I'm sorry for ruining your marriage."

I felt terrible, not for Greg, but for my mom. I hated to see her in pain. Years later, I learned that my mom had filed for divorce and asked Greg to leave the house. I felt like a fool. She soon followed suit, as her presence in our home became less and less frequent.

***

On my first day of high school, I wore a red Timberland shirt and khaki shorts. I was excited to start ninth grade, but being the youngest of three brothers, I was not looking forward to getting hazed as a freshman. Walking to my first class, I heard my name called over the intercom.

Will the young man whose mother doesn't want him please report to the principal's office?

A few staff members stood speaking with a police officer when I walked into the office. The officer turned and faced me.

"You've been listed as a runaway, and a warrant has been issued for your arrest."

"Runaway? I've been home. I'm not a runaway. My mom bought me this outfit for my first day. How many kids run away from home and still show up for school?"

My mom had been on vacation in Mexico for two weeks. She returned home the week before school was scheduled to start and took me shopping for new clothes. Perhaps she felt guilty for not bringing us on vacation with her, but standing there in the office, speaking with a police officer, I realized that she may have had a change of heart. Perhaps she didn't feel so guilty after all. The officer picked up the phone to call her. He put the call on speakerphone and let her know I was in custody.

"What do you want us to do with him?" he asked her.

My mom replied without hesitation.

"Take him away."

Crowds of students looked on as the police walked me out of the high school in handcuffs. The freshman hazing I received from my mom on the first day of school was far worse than anything the other students could've done to me.

I was committed to Edison Detention Center in Doylestown, Pennsylvania. The intake process into the facility included a mandatory strip search and a shower for lice. I refused. The corrections officer begged me to comply, or they would restrain me. I'd barely hit puberty and wasn't comfortable with nudity. The thought of exposing my naked body in front of a grown man terrified me. This was a time in America when young men were taught to fear and hate homosexuality. I sat there for three hours before finally removing my clothes and showering.

The humiliation was unimaginable. Years before, I was forced to remove my pants in front of a room full of women at Assumption B.V.M. after the incident with Greg. This time, I was forced to spread my asscheeks, cough, and then shower nude in front of a strange correctional officer.

Dressed in an orange jumper and Bruce Lee slippers, I carried my bedding folded across my arms as staff escorted me to the chow hall for lunch. We all wore the same outfit, but I was still embarrassed by my appearance. I tried to resist the food but couldn't. With my mom constantly gone, my brothers and I were left unattended for weeks at a time. The fridge was always empty. I would walk back and forth to the kitchen and open the refrigerator door, hoping each time that something had changed. Detention center or not, I gave into my starvation, grateful to eat a hot meal.

That night, I stared at the ceiling in my concrete cell. It was a cold and sleepless episode.

How did my first day of high school turn into my first day in jail?

In the morning, my mom picked me up from the detention center. We rode to school in total silence. She never explained why she had called the police on me.

She dropped me back at school in the same outfit from the day before. The same one I wore as I was escorted down the hall in handcuffs, branding negative recognition upon me.

At the time, my intuition told me that my mom was testing the legal system to see if she could use it to remove me from her home if she wanted to. Apparently, she could. My mom had now discovered the most powerful disciplinary weapon in her arsenal, the police.

6.

After tasting the payoff of the fifty thousand dollar train robbery, I decided to up the ante. Hell, my mom had been trying to send me to jail for the last few years anyway. Never in a million lifetimes would I have thought I'd have enough balls to steal a car, let alone make a career out of it at sixteen years old. Mike and I had our eye on two cars worth almost two hundred thousand dollars, but of course, we had no money to buy them.

We approached the car lot from the back, hopped a fence, and walked onto one of the world's largest dealerships. This particular dealership left the keys in the cars overnight due to the sheer volume of their inventory. All we had to do was make it undetected to the cars we wanted to steal and drive them off the lot. This was still a tough trick to pull off in icy weather with a late-night security guard patrolling the property.

Hiding in the shadows, we located our dream cars and timed out how long it would take for the security guard to loop around the lot.

"What's the plan?" Mike asked.

"Kill the auto headlights, start the car, and put your seat as far back as it will go."

Every time the guard looped around, we drove the vehicles closer to the exit, turning off the engines each time he passed so as not to reveal our presence with the exhaust from the tailpipes. On our third move in the cars, shit luck pulled up behind us. I heard the security guard's car door open. He stepped out and stood motionless fifteen feet from the rear of my car. Seconds became hours as I waited to find out if we were about to get into a high-speed chase or, worse, surrounded by police. My hands gripped the wheel, prepared to run.

Mike looked over at me. Eyes wide, he raised his hands unsure of what to do. I patted the air signaling to get down. I looked in the passenger's side view mirror to check on the guard. Rudolph's red nose appeared, the burning glow of a cigarette.

Two more minutes, and I'm getting the fuck out of here.

After a long moment, he took one last puff, flicked his cigarette butt, and got back into his patrol car.

When he returned to circling the lot we started the cars and drove down to the front entrance. With only a short window of opportunity before he came around again we headed to the exit. That's when I saw it, my worst nightmare.

A brand-new concrete security pole stood between me and my exit. The dealership must have installed the pole sometime between the day we scouted the place and tonight's job. With the clock ticking, it was fourth and goal. I told Mike to get ready to go as I jumped out of my car and into a nearby truck.

The pole sat dead center in front of me between two concrete pillars. A vehicle might narrowly fit. This truck was going to be pushing it. I dropped my foot on the gas and drove straight at it. I was a voluntary crash test dummy. I held my breath, closed my eyes in anticipation, and braced for the impact.

The pole didn't stand a chance. Neither did the mirrors on the truck's sides as I tore through the narrow passageway. The airbags exploded in my face. When I opened my eyes, the truck was wrecked, and our path to escape was clear.

I had a deep admiration for cars. The curves, the history, the speed. I'll never forget the feeling I had that night. It didn't come from stealing the car, almost getting arrested, or the money I would make. It was the rush of escaping from my home life. For once, I was no longer myself but rather someone else, living in a state of wealth and freedom. It was exhilarating.

7.

"Keep your grades up. Don't drink or do drugs. Work hard and stay out of trouble."

Those were the words my dad said to me when my mom dumped me on his doorstep shortly after my release from jail and rocky start to high school. After Fort Dix he moved to Hawthorne, New Jersey, with his girlfriend Barbara. They lived in a small home with train tracks behind it. Power lines buzzed overhead. Aside from a few visits, we hadn't spent much time together since I was a kid.

In the tiny basement of their home for the first time I had my own room. It was too small for a bed, so I slept on a couch in the adjacent room. The TV was only a few feet from where I slept, but I was more than happy to have a bit of privacy.

This was the first time I experienced normal structure in my home life. Barbara made sure that I was comfortable and immediately doted over me. As a family, we sat down for dinner every night and went places together on the weekends. I had chores, a curfew, and weekly responsibilities. Following the rules gave me privileges in my dad's home, and it felt nice to be trusted. I kept my grades up and stayed out of trouble, fulfilling my promise to my dad. I did well with structure, but it wasn't long before cracks began to appear in the delicate facade of my dad and Barbara's everyday life.

One night, I awoke to the sound of an argument from upstairs. I got up from the couch where I slept, slowly snuck to the kitchen entryway, and peeked my head in.

My dad was standing across the room, yelling, hands waving wildly in the air. A lit cigarette traced circles around him. On the table next to a bag of cocaine sat a large stack of money and a bottle of Johnny Walker Black. Barbara was shaking a little under her bobbed haircut but standing her ground. He paced back and forth like a boxer unwilling to return to his stool at the bell.

"Here's your money for the socks!"

In a rage, he scooped up the cash and slapped Barbara in the face with it. Hundred-dollar bills went flying into the air.

"Ten thousand dollars? You're drunk."

Silence filled the room. Embarrassed that the neighbors would hear them arguing I crossed the kitchen and closed the window. In the reflection of the glass, my dad turned and leaned back on the counter to face Barbara. They looked past each other. His anger became sadness.

"I'm sorry how I love you. I'm more sorry how I love drugs."

He left the kitchen and faded down the hallway to their bedroom. I picked up the money off the floor and placed it back on the table beside the cocaine.

Later that night, I lay on the couch in the basement and thought about what I had seen in the kitchen. I realized even though he had moved to a different state, with a woman who loved him, he hadn't changed. The only thing different was that I was old enough to avoid getting burned by his lit cigarettes. I was disturbed and wanted to escape the dysfunction but had no idea how. The clock read four a.m. I had school in three hours. I never looked at my dad the same way again.

***

My first real job was at a catering hall in New Jersey called Macaluso's. I worked late hours after school, making about seven hundred dollars a week. The influx of cash gave me a sense of independence from my dad and kept me on the straight and narrow, at least for a time.

I catered and hosted large events. Everything from weddings to private birthday celebrations. It was nice to watch families celebrate life and love together. I learned a lot about different cultures. Go figure, a Jewish kid working in an Italian catering hall is where I learned the value of family.

Macaluso's gave me unlimited access to liquor, and as my dad's behavior became increasingly erratic, so did mine. I began to spend less time around the house and stayed out late after work, drinking with friends. Gradually, my grades began to slip, and Barbara took notice. I came home early one morning after a long night of drinking to find Barbara alone in the kitchen, waiting for me.

"Your father's in jail."

"What did he do?"

"What didn't he do? Go take a shower. You reek of alcohol."

I can't be entirely certain, but as I went to the bathroom, I thought I heard her mumble under her breath.

"Like father, like son."

***

It was two in the morning when my dad came crashing down the steps into the basement where I slept. His shadowy figure fumbled for the light switch in the dark. I smelled him before I saw him. He stunk of cigarettes, alcohol, and sweat. He finally found the light switch and turned it on.

"It was him or me! Him or me!" he said repeatedly.

His eyes were red, his clothes disheveled, and he was covered in blood. "He was going to shoot me. I had to... I had to."

He rummaged in the basement closet and pulled out hand tools and a power drill. As he rambled on about his most recent near-death experience, he began drilling out the barrel of a revolver in his hand.

Please get him out of here.

"Shut the fuck up! I have to go to school in the morning!" I yelled at the top of my lungs.

Looking back, I can see how my reaction to this situation indicated how quickly I had adjusted to my dad's bizarre behavior. Maybe it was my way of not wanting to confront the ugly reality of what he was involved in. Either way, he didn't appreciate my attitude. The anger poured out of him. He screamed in my face.

"I wish I never had you! You're a fucking replacement baby because your brother died! Your stupid fucking mother is the only reason you're here!"

His spit splattered on my cheek. Even though he was drunk and high, I knew he was telling the truth. He was referring to my brother Jonathan, who had died of SIDS (Sudden Infant Death Syndrome). The reality was that I was a replacement child rather than one born out of love. During my dark days, I'd pray to Jonathan because I knew he was sitting next to God, and for me, that was enough.

My dad disassembled the pistol, turned off the lights mid-rant, and walked back upstairs. It grew quiet. The room was in disarray, covered with the residue of crime, but at least I was left alone with my thoughts.

***

I moved back to Philadelphia on Father's Day, 2000. I was fifteen years old, going on sixteen. Before I left, I gave my dad a bottle of Johnny Walker Black. A show of respect from one man to another. What he said to me while we took shots at the table and played dominoes changed me forever.

"I know what it's like to be alone surrounded by people," he said.

"What do you mean?"

"Son, I know you're not like everyone else. I know you don't fit in. For the rest of your life, you'll always be—" he flipped a blank domino over in his fingers— "pretending to be here."

He filled his glass, raised it in front of his face, and stared into the alcohol as if it was alive and speaking to him then continued.

"Life is rough and unforgiving. I want you to remember when you meet a woman one day that you love, that even if you have nothing, but do something... it can be everything. In the end, we all answer for our sins, but the most important moment to do the right thing in life is when no one is looking."

I wanted to say so many things to him: *Happy Father's Day, I love you—* but I heard Mike honk his horn out front, so all I said was:

"I gotta go."

My dad rarely saw me after that day, but this was our most powerful moment together. I may not have condoned or understood his behavior, but I still loved and forgave him. He was my dad.

Years later, Barbara died from cancer. I never got a chance to thank her for taking care of me that year. I couldn't shake the feeling that her illness might've been caused by the constant buzz of those large power lines that hovered above that little house by the train tracks in Hawthorne, New Jersey.

Mike was waiting outside in the car, engine idling. I loaded the trunk with suitcases full of liquor I'd taken from Macaluso's as an unapproved severance package. I was excited to get back to my old neighborhood and life. Mike drove fast on our way back to Philadelphia as we discussed our plans for summer.

"I planned a welcome home party for you tonight. Girls are coming. Liquor we have, but we need weed. I'll make a quick stop. I know a spot," Mike said.

The view of the city's architecture, as we drove over the Ben Franklin Bridge, gave me a renewed appreciation for the city. Over the past year in

New Jersey, all I thought about were my friends and brothers.

Mike exited the highway and headed to Kensington Avenue. The street was run down, lawless, and decayed. I could have swam laps in the trash that lined the sidewalk, and this part of town was known for its open drug market. He parked on the corner across from a bar.

"Are you coming? Don't be scared," he said.

"Thanks, but no thanks, I'm watching my diet and cutting back on the felonies."

Mike rolled his eyes and got out.

"Back in a sec."

Not a minute after Mike walked into the bar, uniformed and undercover police officers with guns drawn rushed into the bar. It was a raid. A short, stocky bald man in a powder blue jumpsuit burst out the side door, stuffing large bags of weed into his jacket as he fled.

I watched the police chase after the bald man. They tackled him, cuffed him, and walked him back to the bar. That's when two undercover officers noticed me sitting in the passenger seat, watching this all unfold. Mike was still inside the bar when the officers started walking in my direction.

Fuck.

I was a minor with two thousand dollars on me and fifty bottles of liquor in the trunk. There was no point in two people going to jail for the same crime. I jumped into the driver's seat, threw it in reverse, and took the fuck off. With no driver's license and no idea where I was going, I ripped through a drug-infested wasteland to find my way home. It looked like

Mike would be having a welcome home party of his own.

***

That year, I returned to the same high school I was forcibly removed from in handcuffs two years prior. The school had a probation office on-site now because of the constant fighting between students that took place on school premises. The probation office consisted of law enforcement, social workers, case managers, and probation officers.

On my first day of eleventh grade, I was running late for class. As I hustled down the hallway, a voice called out behind me. It was the local probation officer, Jim Jones. He caught up to me and stepped in front of the classroom door, blocking my entry.

"I'm watching you. The moment you slip up, your ass is mine," Jim said.

I burst out laughing.

"Where did you learn that line? *Law and Order*?"

Jim wasn't laughing.

"I know about your past, kid. I'll be waiting for you."

"Today's the only day that matters, handsome," I said.

It was my mom's favorite quote. I liked to say it to adults because it seemed to catch them off guard. Officer Jones knew I came from a broken home, so I tried not to let his comment bother me. After all, Jim wasn't far off the mark.

Shortly after my return to Philadelphia Mike and I pulled off the train robbery and began building our never-ending car collection. If it wasn't tied down, we stole it. A few months into the school year, I was standing at my locker when I was hit with a kidney punch. I spun around and saw Damon, a neighborhood kid who had been harassing me since I moved back from New Jersey. I don't know exactly what his problem was with me, but he didn't like me, and I didn't like him.

Throughout the prior year in New Jersey, my dad had hammered two particular ideas into my head.

"If you fight, be prepared to die, and if you ever find yourself in a Southeast Asian nation, never trust a man who doesn't smoke cigarettes."

I never could figure the second one out. I think he was referring to the Jewish proverb, "Never trust the man who tells you all his troubles but keeps from you all his joys." He might have conflated the Torah with certain ideas he picked up while rifling through the Philippines.

After the fight, I was taken to see the nurse and then escorted to the principal's office. As I sat down, a detective rushed in with four police officers and handcuffed me.

"You're under arrest for simple assault," the detective said.

"I'd like my one phone call," I said.

They agreed and stepped out of the office. My dad picked up the phone, and I told him what happened.

"Dad I didn't start it, but I won't be bullied."

"Good job. Now, when they come back, do not say a fucking word," he said.

Once again, I was committed to the same detention center my mom had sent me to on my first day of high school. I decided to stand up for myself and go to trial. This was my one chance to tell my side of the story. Naively, I believed that if I told the truth that it would be considered. I didn't start the fight, but I was the one who finished it. It made no difference the judge found me guilty.

After the verdict, the sheriffs brought me to a holding cell. I was no longer a kid walking out of the courtroom. Instead, I was a number on a docket sheet in the system that now represented days, months, and years. The probation officer from my school walked into the cell.

"Who's handsome now?" Jim said.

I looked up, but this time, I wasn't laughing.

"I don't care about what happened with Damon. I want information about crimes in your neighborhood. Give me something I can use, and you'll get six months. If not, you're going away for a year."

There was no way I was going to snitch.

8.

As punishment for breaking the law, the probation department recommended that I be committed to Glen Mills Schools. My only alternative was boot camp. Reluctantly, I agreed to meet with a school representative for an interview. Accompanied by the sound of a clock's wasted minutes, I waited alone for an hour in a conference room at the detention center before the door opened.

A large man in athletic apparel sat down across from me. As he reviewed my file, he spat tobacco juice into a plastic bottle.

"Today's purpose is to determine whether you'll be eligible to attend The Glen Mills Schools. Let's begin with what led to your arrest."

"Fighting."

"Would you care to elaborate more on the details of the situation?"

"He swung. I ducked. We fought. He lost."

He crossed his arms and leaned back in his chair.

"And your relationship with your family?"

"I got two brothers."

I refused to give more than the bare minimum. He stopped the interview.

"I feel like we got off on the wrong foot here. Let's start over."

He pulled out a sweating bottle of Diet Coke and cracked it open. I watched in envy as he took a few gulps.

"You know, you're getting a real opportunity here and if you're lucky enough to be accepted, you'll have to complete a full term with no disciplinary problems."

"Like what kind of problems?"

"If you fight or run, there are serious consequences and repercussions. For example, if you run you'll be charged with escape. And serve five years in state prison."

The Diet Coke was hypnotic.

"I'm sorry. Would you like one?"

He placed a Diet Coke and a bag of peanut M&M's on the table. I accepted his olive branch. As I cherished the taste of regular food, he explained the requirements I needed to accomplish in order to graduate from Glen Mills.

"I would like to demonstrate a physical restraint we use on students so you understand the type of behavior expected from you at Glen Mills."

First, he led me to a wall and told me to remain still. He grabbed my shoulders and pressed my chest against the wall using his forearm. Then tackled me to the ground and applied pressure to my torso with his knee while restraining my arms at my sides.

"You okay with this?"

"Okay," I gasped.

"At Glen Mills, we live by cardinal rules. We believe in structure, routine, discipline, but most importantly, education."

I didn't believe a word out of his mouth but felt the need to comply. Despite his use of excessive force, I assumed Glen Mills would be a better option than boot camp.

Immaculately trimmed grass, no fences, no guards. From the outside, it looked like an average college campus in America. Huge brick buildings stood on rolling green fields with bright blue skies in the background. I sat handcuffed in the back of a white van as we drove down a long stretch of road to Glen Mills. Everyone had their shirts tucked in, walked in unison, and waved at our van like robots.

The smell of mold filled my nose as I entered the main hall through a massive set of double doors. Sweat trickled down my forehead as I waited in an old foyer with no central air. I overheard staff talking inside the intake office and peeked inside to see a man with a mullet pointing to a map.

"We need to do more business in this area," said the man with the mullet.

A woman with a beehive hairdo called me into the office for a physical exam by their doctor, who sat at a desk while she stood in the back of the room.

"Take off your clothes," the doctor demanded.

"With her? In here?" I hesitated.

"She's staff," he dismissed. "She's fine."

Frightened and confused I disrobed. She proceeded to ask a series of questions while I was nude. Then handed me a pen and clipboard with papers on it. I had no idea what she wanted me to sign. She saw my hesitation.

"Sign it! Or I will send you back to the detention center!"

Fear forced my hand. I had just committed myself for the next year to this institution. My signature secured my fate.

After I was admitted, staff escorted me down to my designated unit, Jackson Hall. The downstairs consisted of a small sitting area, an office, and a pool table in the back. I was instructed to take off my shoes upon entry. The floor was covered with a thin, brown-grey carpet that left my feet cold. I sat in the common area and was greeted by another student who had been there for a year.

"Name is Getts. I'm your big brother until you get situated. If you need anything or have any questions, come to me. Our counselor's name is Bear."

"Why do they call him Bear?"

"Beats. Everyone's. Ass. Regularly."

It took me a moment to comprehend his acronym.

"Listen, I know you just got here, but you must introduce yourself to every staff member by the end of tonight unless you want to get beat up by them."

I stared at him blankly. Was he fucking with me? I noticed another kid who arrived with me attempt to shake Bear's hand without properly introducing himself. Bear chucked the kid onto the couch and stomped on his chest. The boy let out a high-pitched cry.

Getts wasn't fucking with me.

My first night at Glen Mills felt like an eternity. I wasn't allowed to leave my bed, even to use the bathroom. If I did, it was considered an escape attempt. We were instructed to attack, restrain, and stop any fellow student caught out of bed trying to escape. Only the night staff could permit bathroom usage if they happened to pass by during your time of need. Sometimes, they made rounds, and sometimes, they didn't.

I lay awake in bed, trying to sleep, but my mind raced. The image of that kid being kicked in the chest replayed over and over. When I finally began to drift off, I was awakened by a staff member yelling and kicking my bed.

"On your feet. You have five minutes to use the bathroom and get downstairs."

After a quick headcount to ensure that no one had escaped, we were escorted to the cafeteria. All new students at Glen Mills were subjected to an introductory blackout program. Every movement I now made was controlled. There may have been no fences here, but there also was no freedom.

"Facedown. Foreheads on the table. Don't speak," a staff member commanded.

We were only permitted to raise our heads to eat in silence. Then we cleared our trays, returned to our seats, and placed our heads back down on the table.

When the cafeteria's temperature rose with the sun's heat, they returned us to the housing unit for a town hall meeting. The purpose of these meetings was to deal with issues and conduct head counts. Town hall protocol kept us seated indefinitely in a stress position. We were packed in so tight that the knees of the person behind us dug into our backs. If you broke the uniformed seating arrangement, you were removed and beaten. Even with the excruciating pain in my hips, I remained still and silent. When an emergency town hall was called, it meant no class, food, or activities until the issue was resolved. We were forced into that cramped posture for hours, days, and sometimes weeks.

I was assigned a roommate who was deemed in the language of Glenn Mills to be *problematic*. On more than one occasion, he wet the bed. He wasn't a bad kid, but his nightly requests to staff for the bathroom left him in constant trouble.

"Name's Lenny. Nice to meet you," he said as he entered my room.

"You too. Where are you from?" I asked.

"New Jersey."

I thought about New Jersey.

"Sorry to hear that."

He placed his blanket and a cardboard box on the top bunk. I could see pictures and letters of his family sticking out of his property.

"I have a medical condition," he said nervously.

"Asthma? You snore? What the fuck is it?"

"My mother said it's called urinary incontinence," Lenny said.

I attempted to relate.

"I don't read too good either. I'm incompetent too."

***

At the end of a long conference table, Bear sat reading his newspaper. Behind him was the entrance to the tunnels. Concrete walls loomed behind iron bars that posed as an entryway. I couldn't quite see inside, but the tunnel resembled a dungeon. I knocked on the office door and waited for his acknowledgment.

Bear looked at me as if I had just run over his dog.

"I need some cleaning supplies please."

"Get 'em and get the fuck out."

I gathered what I needed in a bucket, and turned to exit the office.

"Wait," Bear called out. He gestured for me to sit down.

"While you're in here there's a few things we need to discuss. Let's start with your weekend home pass."

Passes were only allowed once a certain level of trust was established due to good behavior. It typically takes students around three months to earn this privilege. I acquired mine in forty-five days. He picked up the phone and dialed my mom.

As he spoke, I drifted off. Getts had warned me about the tunnels. They were originally used to facilitate the movement of children underground at Glen Mills but now served only one purpose: punishment. Their conversation faded. I tuned into the underworld. I heard the ghost of a thousand broken households in that tunnel. Bear slapped the table. The voices ceased to exist.

After a brief exchange, Bear hung up the phone. I saw a look on his face that I had never seen before. Maybe I was reading too much into his expression, but I swore I saw a momentary flicker of compassion.

"You're not going home. Your mother denied your pass."

Given our damaged relationship, I wasn't surprised, but I could not understand how she would deny me a visit with my brothers. I suppose I'd have to wait for another day. Surely, the holidays would bring me better fortune.

***

Three days later I found myself back in that office.

Bear slid a newspaper across the table. The veins in his neck bulged.

"Are you illiterate Lenny?"

"I can read, sir," Lenny replied.

"Show me."

Lenny opened the newspaper, held it close, and squinted. He had vision problems on top of all of his other medical issues. He struggled to read aloud as the paper fluttered in his hands.

Bears punch tore a hole through the newspaper and knocked Lenny clean out of his chair.

Bear looked at me.

"If Lenny gets out of bed at night to pee, beat his ass." "What?" I was dumbfounded.

"Tell. Lenny. You will beat his ass if he gets out of bed again."

It was an incredibly awkward moment. I looked down at Lenny.

"I'll fuck you up if you get out of bed."

"Do you understand, Lenny?" Bear said.

"Yes, sir." he choked through tears.

"Now. Get your ass up and go stand in front of town hall for feedback. You're in an issue for disrespecting staff and pissing the bed."

Lenny stood in front of the students who looked on from their routine stress positions. Students in issues were referred to by staff as *peons* and forced to receive feedback. Staff encouraged emphasis on the "p" to make sure spit landed in the offending student's face. If feedback didn't work these so-called peons were forced inside of those tunnels in the back of that main office. Lenny now found himself in the crosshairs of a verbal firing squad.

Staff chose students who disliked Lenny to give him feedback that degraded him. They spit and yelled in his face so loud that he flinched. Flinching was strictly forbidden. He attempted to regain his composure, but the staff beat him so severely that he peed himself. This time, it was in front of everyone.

"Who's Lenny's roommate?" a senior staff member called out.

I raised my hand.

"Escort him upstairs before lights out so he can shower."

I broke formation and rose. Lenny looked up at me from the floor. He shook his head as if to say no, and that he was defeated. I nodded yes, to encourage him to get up. Few times in life I've seen a man reach his breaking point. This was one of them. As roommates, we had many late-night conversations about growing up in Philadelphia. I prayed my facial expression was enough to remind Lenny of one conversation in particular.

How do you do it? How do you never let anything bother you? Lenny had asked.

If you let them break you, then they win.

He grabbed the edge of the couch and staggered to his feet. Lenny dug deep. He brushed himself off, straightened his clothes, and walked tall out of the town hall meeting.

We walked back to our room together. I broke the silence.

"Don't worry man, I'm not going to fight you if you need to use the bathroom."

Lenny looked at me. I saw the relief in his eyes.

"You know what to do when life hands you lemons?"

"Make lemonade?" He asked.

"Well, in this case... Urinade."

At the next town hall meeting, it was announced that Lenny was granted permission to use the bathroom at night. Wherever Lenny is today, I hope he's healed from the abuse he suffered during his time at Glen Mills.

***

Ten long months had passed before my mom finally allowed me to come home for Thanksgiving. When I arrived, my brothers greeted me with a double hug. I didn't want to let go. It was a much-needed breath of fresh air to be reunited with my family. It felt like I hadn't seen them in forever. We spent the day at my mom's house around the table, eating, laughing, and reminiscing over good times. After dinner, my brothers and I went to celebrate at a neighborhood holiday party.

Weed and alcohol were scattered throughout the house, with random kids using plenty of both. Loud music played into the late hours of the night. The noise level made me uneasy, and being home on supervised leave didn't help either. I was worried someone was going to call the cops. After a few hours of watching kids drink and smoke, I'd had enough.

I looked for my brothers to say goodbye. I saw Sammy in the crowd first. I cautioned him about drinking and driving. Call it intuition.

"If you get fucked up, promise me you won't drive."

We hugged.

"I promise, buddy," Sammy said.

I followed the sound of laughter and found Vinny at a poker table surrounded by friends and cocaine. A true gambler, he was taking everyone's money.

"Hold up, I'll walk home with you," Vinny offered. He poured one last shot.

"Good night losers. You can all thank Cinderella here for saving your asses," he celebrated triumphantly and threw back his shot.

Along the walk, I told him about my horrific experiences at Glenn Mills. He was shocked.

"Don't worry, dude. There will come a day when you walk out of there."

Vinny noticed my unorthodox behavior and looked at me with confusion.

"What the fuck are you doing?"

I realized I had been waving at every passing car like a robot. The rules of Glen Mills had become my life. I'd been in a bad remake of *The Truman Show*, except in my movie, no audience watched, and no crew members kept us safe.

Early the next morning, the sound of fists pounding on my front door echoed throughout the house. Through my bedroom window, I saw a cop car parked in the street as two police officers stood on my front porch. Even though I hadn't done anything wrong, I assumed the police were there for me. My mom opened the door, spoke with the officers briefly, and invited them inside. I hid behind a dresser at the top of the stairs and eavesdropped in on their conversation.

"Your son's been involved in a car accident. We need you to come to the hospital with us please," the officer said.

"What happened?" my mom asked.

"Your son was in a car accident early this morning out on Route 13. He's in the ICU. Unfortunately, we don't know anything further at this time."

A part of me remembers my mom collapsing in tears, but I can't be sure. I have gaps in my memory when it comes to this moment in my life. The entire family jumped in the car and rushed to Frankford Torresdale Hospital.

When we arrived, the doctor spoke with my mom in the waiting room while we surrounded her. The news was devastating.

"Your son wasn't wearing his seat belt. He was ejected from the car through the windshield. The driver fell asleep at the wheel and drove into a tree. Sadly, the driver was killed on impact. Your son was revived on the scene, and he's now in critical condition."

Sammy was the toughest guy I knew. I assumed he was banged up and bruised, but that's not what I saw when I walked into his room. Both of his eyes were swollen shut. He lay unconscious stretched out on the bed, tubes connected to every part of his body. I wanted to hold him but couldn't. He suffered a severe brain injury, broken bones, and a fractured spine. He spent several days in a coma. It was my fault. I should've never left him at that party.

When he finally woke up, he was unable to speak. The expression on his face was of confusion, disorientation, and coming back from the dead. His jaw was wired shut, and he moaned in agony. I never imagined being in this scenario. I assumed he would brush himself off and get right back in the game, but I learned that life doesn't play fair. He spent the next several years unable to speak, eat, or do anything without assistance. My heart broke for my brother.

The doctors initially misdiagnosed Sammy's spinal injury, which led to further complications and permanent paralysis. He would never walk again and his accident left him in need of constant care and attention for the rest of his life. This was the second time Sammy was involved in an accident on Thanksgiving. Both times, he lost a friend. This time, I lost my brother.

Sammy wasn't dead, but our lives would never be the same. He wouldn't be there to teach me how to talk to girls at school. We'd never play football in the park again. There would be no more riding bikes together. I thought if I held onto the belief that these things would happen again, then everything would be all right. This couldn't be the end of our story. That day, my world collapsed, but this was still nothing compared to what my brother was going through. He was a prisoner in his own body.

***

Upon my return to Glen Mills, there was no dread, there was no anxiety. There were two types of kids at Glen Mills. Those who bought into the bullshit and those who didn't. We wore the same clothes and ate the same food, but I guess my dad was right, I was only pretending to be here.

A few weeks later, my probation officer, Jim Jones, intervened and advocated for my release from Glen Mills.

In April 2019, The Glenn Mills Schools was shut down amidst multiple allegations of sexual and physical assault dating back decades. Students were conditioned to believe violent discipline was provided for our benefit. Speaking about what transpired during our collective incarceration was forbidden. Everything I had witnessed was confirmed by the former students who came forward and spoke out.

The Glen Mills staff told me I had graduated from their program and discharged me out front of the same courthouse where I'd been convicted and sentenced one year before. I didn't graduate from Glen Mills Reform Schools. I survived.

9.

Upon my release from Glen Mills, I decided to be a productive member of society. A friend of a friend hired me for a job at a local car dealership. On my first day at work, I woke up on time and made a strong cup of coffee. The forecast called for clear skies and sunshine. It was going to be a good day. I ironed a crease into a new pair of black pants and put on a crisp polo shirt with a hat bearing the logo of my new employer. I left the house and went to catch the seven-fifteen bus downtown. If you're not ten minutes early, you're late.

The bus dropped me off at the corner of the parking lot at eight fifty on the dot. I was right on time. I noticed an empty bottle on the ground near the entrance of the car dealership. I picked it up and tossed it in the trash can. An older woman was approaching to enter the building. I waited and held the door open for her.

"Thank you," she said.

I smiled. "You're welcome, young lady."

I wiped my feet on the welcome mat and looked for the detailing bay.

"Good morning, Susie," I said to the receptionist as I walked past her desk. Susie looked at me blankly.

"... ... good morning, sir?"

I breezed through the lobby, took a quick look to see who was in, and headed toward the detailing bay. The general manager briefly stopped me. He was a bit confused about who I was, but he was friendly and welcomed me to the team.

The shop was filled with people prepping and detailing the cars to be picked up. No time to waste, I went through the order list, pulled the slip I needed, and retrieved the keys. According to the order, a customer was coming for that specific car within the next hour. I didn't want to be responsible if the customer got upset, nor be caught red-handed slacking on the job. Especially on my first day. My boss walked up to me and looked at my name tag.

"Who are you?" he asked.

"I just started today. My name is Gian. The GM sent me to prep a vehicle for an important customer. I have fifteen minutes before they arrive. I need the keys for a black Cadillac STS-V, please."

The manager grabbed the car keys from the rack and tossed them to me.

"Thank you, back in a flash," I said.

I hurried to the lot and looked for the car that matched the invoice. The car was fully loaded. This should be fun. I pressed the button on the key fob to unlock the doors. Lights flashed. *Bingo*!

The detailing process for a fifty-thousand-dollar car is essential. Only pure professionalism will make the grade. First, you scrape off the window decals, attach a temporary license plate, and gas it up before slipping on white gloves to wipe off all the smudges and fingerprints.

My manager was standing out front with the GM by the entrance. Perfect. They'll get one last chance to see how well I detailed the car before it leaves. I drove past them slowly into the pick-up area. Instead of stopping at the pickup area, I thought it would be best to continue creeping forward toward the exit of the lot.

When I looked in the rearview mirror, I saw the GM and my manager waving their hands wildly.

"Stop! Stop!" they yelled.

The GM began jumping up and down. My manager broke into a sprint. I continued off the lot without slowing down. I turned right, waved at them, and drove away.

Armed with only a company hat, shirt, and a smile. I managed to pull off this heist with a criminal's most underestimated attribute, charm. As they say, drive it like you stole it. Well, I actually did.

***

I was seventeen years old the first time I tried a prescription pill. After my horrific year at Glen Mills, I came home to an empty house. Vinny had moved out, Sammy was in the hospital, and my mom was hardly around. She was working nights and seeing a new boyfriend. I felt like the last man standing.

I wanted to feel like a typical teenager again. I went to a party with my buddies and was offered Xanax. It's only one. How bad could it be?

After leaving the party, I felt the Xanax kick in while I drove home. My eyelids grew heavy as I got closer to my neighborhood. I struggled to stay awake. I made it home, but I never left the car. I fell asleep in the driveway with the engine running.

Sammy and I were in the backyard playing baseball. It was a full count. I wound up and threw a fastball down the middle. Smack! With the crack of the bat, the baseball came right back at me and hit me in the face. Pain ripped through my jaw, and the impact knocked me off the mound, but the ball hit me again before I could react.

Smack. Smack. Smack. Smack.

***

I opened my eyes, still in the driver's seat of my car. Punches rained down on my face. The blows came from every direction, thumping into my skull. The drugs, combined with the beating, left me unable to move. My instincts finally kicked in. I battled through the haze of Xanax, overriding the disorientation.

The car door stood open. A crushing weight pinned me to the seat. The shoelace on my right sneaker became hooked under the gas pedal. I thrashed wildly and struggled to break free. My attacker punched me in the face until he ran out of breath, take a break, and then punched me some more. Blood poured from the top of my head and ran into my eyes. I knew I would die if I didn't leave that car. I pulled with all my might and snapped the shoelace, breaking my foot free from the gas pedal.

"What the fuck do you want!" I screamed.

"Money," he said.

"I have money in the house. I'll go inside and get it for you," I said.

He yanked me out of the car, and I fell to my knees. I stood up and looked my attacker in the face. I knew who he was now. He punched me again.

"If I have to come inside, I'll fucking kill you."

I stumbled around the side house and went to the basement window. I kicked it in and fell head-first into the pitch-black. Blinded by blood, I felt my way through the darkness. I climbed the stairs and went for the phone to call 911, but my mom had ripped the phone cord out of the wall so many times that the wiring was destroyed. The absurdity of the situation suddenly struck me, and I laughed. For the first time, I *wanted* the police to come to my house. I wasn't going to die from the attack. I was going to die because I couldn't get a fucking dial tone.

A ringing sound grew louder and more high-pitched. Vibrations of pain faded and then evaporated my equilibrium. I fumbled with the wires in the dark. I felt consciousness slipping. A streetlamp poked its glow through the window. I leaned into the light to see better. Face half-lit, my fingertips were slick with blood. I squinted with my one good eye but struggled to find the wire in the darkness.

Bile rose in my throat. With one last lurch, I clutched the phone cord and focused my vision. The jack swam before me enticingly from the shadows. *One more pitch, Sammy.* Sammy's bat exploded on contact. Shards of wood floated across the dial tone of my consciousness.

I awoke to sunlight shining through a window. I winced against the brightness. An ECG machine beeped next to me. Every beep of that machine was a thunderclap in my skull. I was in a hospital bed. I tried to sit up, but couldn't. Sleep paralysis stopped me, or so I thought. The tension on my wrist then became apparent. I was handcuffed to the bed. A doctor entered the hospital room.

"You need to rest," he said.

"I have to use the bathroom."

A police officer came into the room and uncuffed my wrist. As I staggered to the bathroom, he stood by the bed and watched me. I closed the bathroom door behind me.

I looked into the mirror and saw the reflection of a person standing behind me. Startled, I spun around, but no one else was there. My face was smashed in so severely that I didn't recognize myself.

What is the purpose of life? Mine seems to have no value.

At first, I was sad, but then a fit of short-lived anger struck me. The room began to vibrate, I vomited and blacked out.

Why am I here?

I woke up back in the hospital bed, handcuffed again. The police officer was seated in a chair by the door.

"Why am I here?" I asked.

The officer replied, "I'm here to take you into custody once you're cleared to leave."

After a battery of tests, I was taken back to my room. Later that evening, a new doctor came in and introduced himself. We reviewed my test results together.

"Do you recall being hit with a pipe?"

"No."

"You were most likely beaten with a weapon. Another blow to the head might have killed you."

He went on to explain that I may have permanent loss of feeling in my lip, a speech impediment, and paralysis on the left side of my face.

"You will most likely suffer from migraines for the rest of your life."

"So what's the bad news, Doc?"

I had an orbital fracture, a hyphema in my left eye, severed nerves in my face, a severe concussion, and multiple contusions on my head. Due to the seriousness of my injuries, the doctors opted not to release me. I would be staying overnight for observation.

That evening was a drug-induced nightmare brought on by morphine. A warm rush ran through my veins. My mind's eye was a bizarre swirl of phantom attackers and surrealist imagery. A shadow hovered over my hospital bed. Odor in the dark. The beautiful mystique of the drug whispered to me.

"Enjoy the ride."

My car stood empty in the abyss. Windows broken, tires slashed. I crossed the threshold. Alone in the driver's seat, I buoyed in an ocean of black. A vanilla moon hung overhead. Handcuffed to the steering wheel, the car doors were gone. Oily water rushed in. The taste of iron, the smell of flesh. Death was a fashionable idea.

***

The sheriffs escorted me through the main lobby to the elevator and brought me upstairs to be arraigned. I sat in the defendant's chair. The judge read off a list of charges.

"Count One, attempted murder. Count Two, possession of a deadly weapon. Count Three, drive-by shooting."

Had the morphine gotten the best of me? Was this another dark vision?

I knew it was real when they read the charges aloud for a second time. How was it possible that I, the person who was almost murdered, was now being charged with attempted murder myself? It turned out that while I was hospitalized, somebody shot up the house of my attacker. The prosecution was trying to leverage a case on me.

"Your Honor, clearly the defendant had the motive to retaliate against his attacker given the—"

"Young man, where have you been for the last forty-eight hours?" the judge interjected.

"I was in the hospital and then taken into custody by the authorities."

The judge dismissed the case due to my current state and the fact that I was in custody at the time of the drive-by shooting. He stated that it was physically impossible for me to have committed the crime.

I couldn't believe my life was teetered on the brink of destruction on accusations alone. The man who had attacked me was a close friend of

Damon's. His face was branded in my mind. I could only deduce that this was a retaliation for the conflict that landed me in Glen Mills.

After the hearing, I was released and headed to the elevator to leave. I ran into my former probation officer, Jim Jones. He joined me on the way down to the first floor. He saw that I was shaken up about being falsely accused of a crime.

"Kid, are you all right?"

Am I still a kid?

Seeing my condition, he offered me a ride to my brother's house in Northeast Philly. Even though he was my probation officer, I never felt that this man was truly my enemy, so I accepted the ride.

My head pounded as Jim spoke to me. *Hotel California* played in the background as he drove south on Interstate 95. He said he was in the courtroom during my arraignment. We talked about my life and the recent events that had landed me beside him in the elevator that morning.

When I arrived at my brother's house, I shook his hand, said thanks, and stepped out of the car. As I began to walk away, he rolled down the window and called out to me. I stopped and turned around, squinting against the sun.

"I'm sorry I didn't believe you sooner," Jim said.

"Believe me about what?"

"About everything."

"I wouldn't have believed me either."

The night of the attack, I was found on my back, surrounded by a halo of blood, in a state of asphyxiation. The combination of Xanax, the concussion, and liquor had nearly killed me. I guess my attacker meant what he said about coming in after me, but failed to cover his tracks upon leaving. One of my neighbors happened to be passing by in the early morning and noticed my front door in disarray. If that neighbor had never called the police I would've died that night. This was most definitely childhood's end.

SUMMER

10.

The way my life had unfolded thus far, I assumed that I would be dead by the age of twenty-five. I lived on the red line. My general rule of thumb was to multiply the speed limit by two. When I stole a car, the confines of the institutions that had come to define my life came crashing down. The truth of speed set me free.

As I approached the intersection on the hunt for freedom, red lights shined above a fading yellow apparition. I painted the town green. I was armed with four wheels, two doors, and zero fucks given about tomorrow.

Two pretty girls pulled up next to my car. They waved over at me. I revved back. We smiled. I was barely eighteen with five hundred horses under my foot.

"Who's your friend?" the driver asked, nodding with her head towards the shadowy figure riding shotgun.

"Don't worry about him. He's a real dummy," I replied.

The music that blasted from their car windows became a part of my life's never- ending soundtrack. Brakes locked, I spun my tires like black vinyl records, volume up, pedal down. Clouds of smoke poured from my tires, enveloping the intersection.

"Meet us at Blue Martini!" the driver yelled as she turned the corner and drove away.

My public display of flirting had attracted some unwanted attention— the police. White lights shined in front of me as blue and red flashed from behind. Self- control and discipline took a back seat as the need for speed and adrenaline took the wheel. I was an outlaw, wide awake, and blazing through the American dream.

Unlike the dummy seated next to me, the best chance I had of getting away was to add distance between myself and the police, and then immediately abandon the vehicle. I looked down at the options on the gear shifter.

P, R, N,

D, P, D.

Park, Reverse, Neutral, Drive, Prison, or Death.

I made a hard right down the wrong-way street in life and blew past oncoming traffic down my favorite quarter-mile stretch in Philly. The good die young, and my passenger was a very, very good guy. He wore a Mike Schmidt Jersey with the number twenty on the back.

"Everyone, please meet John. John, this is everyone. Everyone, don't get too attached to your new friend, as he won't be here for long."

The lighter fluid fumbled in my hands. I struggled a bit, then I lit John on fire. Flames poured freely from the open window as I accelerated to my exit point.

The woods began thirty yards away from where the pavement hit the grass. I jumped the curb, ripped the emergency brake, and slid across the open field like a hockey puck on ice. My hi-beams now faced the police, blinding them. I hopped out.

"Help!" I yelled.

As the cops rushed to extinguish the marshmallow mannequin roasting in the passenger seat, I disappeared into the woods. By the time they figured out what had happened, I'd be up in smoke, like the dummy I had left behind. John was gone. So was I. The getaway wasn't the hardest part about the chase. I'd outrun them with ease. It was getting the damn lighter fluid open while driving with my knees. It was time to celebrate, and Blue Martini sounded perfect.

***

I pulled up to the valet and was given the same look as always. Who's that, and where the fuck did he get that car? I proceeded past the line to the front of the bar, slipped the doorman a hundred, and walked inside past the crowd.

Blue Martini was buzzing. I looked around the bar and took it all in. Men wearing too much cologne. Women wore too little clothing. Perspiration, empty glasses, cigarette smoke, and inane conversations about the latest episode of the *Sopranos*.

I noticed a woman at the bar wearing a tight blue dress. She attempted to grab the bartender's attention by waving cash in the air. Ten minutes later, she was still a pedestrian in New York, upstreaming a cab.

Slipping through the crowd, I found my way to the rear of the bar. A waiter passed me with drinks in his hand. This was my way in. Mr. Franklin, work your magic. When the signal in my hand turned green, he stopped.

"Do me a favor," I said, handing him money.

"What's that?" he replied after he took it.

"Go to the bartender, give him one of those bills, and tell him to come over here, please."

The bartender appeared in front of me moments later.

"What can I do for you?" he asked.

"You see that young lady in the blue dress."

He looked back across the bar.

"Take care of her first and meet me with a double shot of Hennessy and two Heinekens when I sit alongside her."

He nodded in agreement.

"You got it."

I watched as he walked directly to her and served her a drink. When she tried to pay, he refused her and went on to the next person. I sat down on her right.

"That was a long wait. I'm surprised you stuck it out" I said.

She looked me up and down, "Have you been at the beach?"

I wore a white dress shirt, grey suit, navy blue tie, and black shoes. I had gone home to change after lighting the car on fire, but I didn't have time to shower.

"Do I look like I'm dressed for the beach?" I quipped.

"No, but you smell like a bonfire."

Her comment made me realize that she was the driver of the car I had flirted with at the intersection earlier that night.

"No bonfire. I was just roasting a marshmallow."

I threw back my shot. The bartender looked at her and nodded toward me.

"Thank you for the drink," she said as she extended her hand, "Lana. Nice to meet you."

I took her hand and said, "Nice to meet you, Lana."

"I see your suit matches your car. Nice watch."

Glad that she noticed, I said, "Thank you, it's a Rolex."

"A real man knows it's not the value of the watch, but the value of his time." She sounded unimpressed.

I wouldn't truly grasp the meaning of her remark until years later. By then, it would be too late.

"Oh yeah, why's that?" I said.

"You seem to have everything you need, but still haven't figured it out."

Her comment caught me off guard, so I decided to zing her back.

"Says the woman with a Chanel handbag."

"Well, at least you're not a pushover," she said.

She told me a little about herself. Her dad was a workaholic with a bad temper. He left Lana's mother for another woman when she was twelve. Her mother was a nurse who took her to foreign countries every summer to do volunteer medical care, which led her to pursue a career in nursing herself. We spoke for a while before she turned the conversation to me.

"So what about you? You drive a nice car, dress well, and you're handsome, but too young to be a lawyer or doctor. Let me guess, pharmaceutical rep?"

"Please don't disrespect me," I laughed. "I would never poison the masses with *prescription* drugs."

The key word was prescription.

As she sipped her drink, I locked eyes with her, grinned like an idiot, and whispered like it was a secret between us. "I'm part of a multi-national car theft organization."

She laughed so hard that she almost spit her drink out. Meeting someone I actually wanted to get to know was unexpected. Her story made me feel embarrassed about the way I lived my life. She was dedicated to helping people, and I was committed to breaking the law. I couldn't help but feel ashamed.

"I know you're a woman who values her time, but would you be willing to share some of yours with me?"

She wrote down her number on a napkin with an eyeliner pen, kissed it, and handed it to me.

"You better not waste it."

11.

By the time I was eighteen, I had stolen over two million dollars worth of cars, but unfortunately, the wheelman only gets a small slice of the profit. I knew I was lucky to have escaped all the police chases and started to question my high- stakes lifestyle.

Stealing cars paid the bills, but I wanted real money. I decided to try hustling, but I needed investment capital and a connection. I knew I would have to go to the West Coast, Mexico, or Canada to find a consistent supplier. How would I find the people who didn't want to be found? I had no idea, but I knew it would take networking and determination.

Nothing travels faster in Philly than word of mouth. Information came my way about a drug dealer who had been arrested and was being held in booking downtown.

A little birdie told me that the dealer being detained downtown owned a warehouse in South Philly, serving as a stash spot for dirty cash. I had to act fast, with the window of opportunity closing in less than two days. The birdie advised me not to walk through the door if I wasn't prepared to deal with the potential consequences on the other side. I weighed the odds. It was risky, but I thought it could be enough money to change my life. The job would be simple: steal a car, get in, get the cash, get out. It's never that simple.

Around eight o'clock, the sun went down, and the rain began to pour. It was a boiling summer night, and the rain pumped up the humidity. I parked around the back of the warehouse, rolled down the window, and listened. Aside from the rain and the faint noise of traffic over Interstate 95, I heard nothing.

Two cameras, one on each corner, covered the sides of the building. I made my way through a blind spot between the cameras and entered through a small window that faced a wooded area in the back of the building.

The window brought me into a hallway that accessed the stairwell. There were no infrared sensors in the building. Basic magnetic alarms were connected to the main doors and windows. Simple.

I headed up to the third floor and approached the office cautiously. I needed to access the wall beyond a large wooden door with a magnetic sensor at the top. I broke out a sledgehammer, crowbar, and portable circular saw. I placed small wedges into the door frame to alleviate vibrations that might trip the sensor and set off an alarm.

I flipped the red switch on the circular saw and began to cut a hole in the bottom half of the door. Wood chips kicked back into my face like shell casings on a semi-automatic handgun.

I poked my head through the hole in the door and spotted my target. I crawled through the opening and crept over to the wall behind the filing cabinets across the room. I tossed the cabinets aside and smashed holes in the wall with the sledgehammer. Nothing came loose. No large sums of cash.

In the heat of the moment, I began to doubt my source. Maybe the birdie needed better information. I looked around the rest of the office. I found a small room in the back with a coffee machine, office supplies, and a large safe. I wasn't prepared to take on a job this big and I didn't have the tools with me to crack this thing. The clock was ticking. I grew frustrated. I called the birdie.

"There's nothing here, asshole! The money is in a safe!" I said.

"It's not in the safe, that's a decoy. Are you sure you are at the right wall?" the birdie asked.

"Yes, I'm fucking sure!"

"It's there. Smash down every wall if you have to."

I hung up the phone, and like Mr. Gorbachev in 1989, I tore down this wall. The demolition charge was a madman armed with a sledgehammer. White powder from the impact of steel against drywall exploded everywhere. Covered in wall fragments, I looked like I'd taken a kilo of cocaine to the face. Sure as shit, the birdie was right.

In the back corner of the office, wedged between two frames inside the wall, vacuum-sealed bundles of cash were stacked from the floor to the ceiling. I didn't know how much it was, but it was a lot. I shoved the cash into a black canvas bag, loaded the tools, and took... the fuck... off.

From the window at the top of the stairs on the third floor, I could see the lights of two cop cars driving toward the front of the building. Someone must have heard me reciting Ronald Reagan's famous speech behind those filing cabinets.

I bolted down a set of stairs that led to the rear of the building. I turned and sprinted to the exit, slamming through the double doors at full force, half expecting the police to be waiting for me outside. The coast was clear. With the police coming in from the front, I had just enough time to slip out the back.

I emerged into the rain, heart pumping, racing full speed toward a neighboring apartment complex. Branches clawed at me as I pushed through the thicket. I kept my head down to shield my eyes from impalement. I couldn't see the helicopter, but I could hear the propeller in the distance. They were closing in. I chucked the bag of tools into the woods.

Dead weight. I'll buy new ones. I knew this job was a bad idea. It's never that simple!

I threw the duffle bag of cash over the fence. Then leaped over, and tore off my black drywall-covered shirt to reveal the grey one I wore underneath it. I put on a hat, picked up the bag, and regained my composure.

I walked from the back parking lot to the front of the building. I desperately needed to get inside. I located the intercom and buzzed every apartment in the building. Heavily accented English emerged from the speaker.

"Yes?"

"Mr. Chow's Chinese delivery," I said, catching my breath.

"I have no order. Please delete me."

"Can you buzz me in, please?"

"Delete my apartment building," the voice squawked.

"What?"

"Delete my inventory!"

Fuck!

"Delete me now!"

One of the random tenants hit the button. The door buzzed open. Thank God, I slid inside.

The elevator reeked of urine and fecal matter. I gagged as I descended to the basement. I hustled down a dark corridor and looked over my shoulder before I entered the laundry room.

The smell of mold and dryer sheets filled the air. I barricaded the door with a large trash can and door stopper to keep it shut. This was it, the moment I had been waiting for. I laid the duffle bag on top of the washing machine and slid open the zipper.

Stacks of neatly bundled twenties, fifties, and hundreds filled the bag. I pulled out a box cutter and sliced open one of the bags. I flipped through one of the stacks of cash. The edge of the bundle sounded like the wings of a tiny hummingbird. At a glance, it looked to be around half a million. I now had the start-up cash I needed to get away from stealing cars and become a full-blown hustler. Still soaked, I opened up a dryer and looked for a sweater or shirt big enough to fit me. A black shirt and brown corduroy jacket would have to do. I threw my wet grey shirt into the trashcan and got changed. I took five hundred dollars out of the duffle bag and tossed it into the dryer. It's one thing to steal someone's ill-gotten gains, but it's another thing to take the clothes off a man's back.

I cracked open the basement door and stepped outside. The rain had stopped, and the air was fresh. I looked to the skies.

12.

A massive glass high-rise building stood in front of me. One month had passed since the night of the robbery. I snapped my head forward and looked straight ahead as two enormous glass doors inhaled me into a grand lobby. I approached the concierge's desk.

"I'm here to see DaVinci."

I wasn't sure if they were going to laugh me out the front door.

"One moment, please."

A call was made, and a few words were exchanged in a hushed tone, followed by a brief pause. The concierge looked up at me.

"Right this way, sir."

We walked through one of the most impressive lobbies I've ever seen. It looked like an art museum.

Who was this guy?

I stood waiting for the elevator, listening to the dings as it approached the lobby. The concierge reached in and pressed the button for the penthouse floor.

"Third door on the right. Have a nice day, sir."

My mind raced as I ascended. My ears popped at the same time the doors did.

I made my way down the hall, but the door opened before I could knock.

Two men the size of refrigerators stood in the dimly lit foyer. One looked angry; the other looked angrier.

"Lifft yohl arums," one of them uttered, with an accent that made him sound like a terrorist from *Die Hard*.

I raised my arms, and they patted me down.

"Fallow zee hallway down to zee main room. He's waiting fuhl you."

Framed photographs signed by celebrities and other business associates lined the hallway. DaVinci seemed to know everybody from movie stars to musicians. The list went on and on, but one particular photo stopped me in my tracks. It was George Jung and DaVinci dressed casually, holding whiskey glasses. It looked like they were standing in someone's backyard.

For those of you who have never heard of George Jung, he was one of the most notorious drug dealers of all time. George started as a small-time pot dealer who then graduated to smuggling large amounts of marijuana from Mexico to the United States. He was also known for shipping planeloads of cocaine from Columbia to Miami in the 1980s. Hollywood produced a film starring Johnny Depp about his career called *Blow*.

Words cannot explain the feeling that came over me as I stood in DaVinci's high- rise condo, looking at that photo of him and George. I knew my life was about to change forever. I looked down toward the living room and saw a man I assumed was DaVinci. He was on the phone.

"Prices just went up," was all I heard him say.

I entered the living room and looked around. Vinny had arranged the meeting with DaVinci, but I hadn't even noticed he wasn't there because I was so distracted by what was in front of me. The condo had floor-to-ceiling windows with a breathtaking cityscape. I had to touch the glass to realize I wasn't looking at a painting. Whoever said crime doesn't pay must not have seen the inside of this guy's home.

He looked at me, said, "*¿Qué onda, güey?*" and pointed to the couch.

The couch was a pristine white leather. I felt bad sitting on it. The coffee table was stacked with books on art, fashion, history, and philosophy. He hung up the phone.

"Your brother tells me you're looking for a new opportunity."

"That's correct."

"So what is it that you do now?"

"A little of this, a little of that, but I'm sure you already know that."

"Do you have any tattoos?"

"Nope, none at all."

"What do you know about men?"

I stared at him, bewildered. "... Excuse me—?"

"—How do you feel about Chinese prisons?"

Before I could even process the questions, Vinny walked into the room.

"I see you fellas have met," Vinny said as he lit a cigarette and sat down beside me on the couch.

"No identifying marks," DaVinci said as he walked to the window. "That means you're worth more money, and there is a lot of money to be made here."

I continued to listen.

"Tony is not Pablo."

I was unsure of what he meant.

"Tony Montana was fictional. Pablo Escobar was real. We are men of flesh and blood. Make no mistake. There is a great difference."

"Why exactly am I here?"

My brother interjected, "You need somewhere to invest your money, and DaVinci needs security and a driver."

"No thanks, bro. I don't drive for anyone but myself."

I was nobody's sucker and damn sure not an errand boy. I thought this meeting was for an investment opportunity. I stood up to leave. DaVinci stood by the window looking out into the city. Without turning around, he said, "You have major potential, but it won't go anywhere unless you learn to ask for help."

Unsure how to respond, I looked at my brother and shrugged. He nodded towards DaVinci.

"How much do you make in a year?" DaVinci asked.

He turned around and looked me straight in the eyes.

"Not enough," I said.

DaVinci's cell phone rang. Without breaking eye contact, he silenced it, and said "What you make in one year, I make in one night."

My eyes flickered to my brother, then back to DaVinci. I stared at him. Money or no money, I still had to look into his eyes and know if I could trust him.

"You can never negotiate from a position of vulnerability. I take it we have a deal?" he said.

DaVinci had me sold, even before I said yes. In an attempt to match his caliber, I replied, "The brave chase dreams, as the tolerant look on."

DaVinci threw me his phone.

"You start tonight."

"I have some business to attend to," I said.

"Not anymore. All the crimes you were involved in before this moment are finished. It's over, you work for me now."

Vinny looked at me.

"Trust him."

That's all I needed to hear to commit to this. I had to take a shot at something new. I couldn't continue to live my life in a perpetual high-speed chase.

DaVinci walked over and shook my hand. I looked at his arm and noticed a koi fish tattoo peeking out from under the sleeve of his shirt.

"There's a suitcase by the door. Take it with you," DaVinci said.

My brother and I walked to the door and made our way back down through the elevators and into the lobby.

"Why do they call him DaVinci?" I asked my brother as we walked out the lobby doors and into the street.

"Because he painted the Mona Lisa."

I shot him a look.

We got in my car together and sat down to talk in private. Vinny opened the glove box, pulled out a CD case, and dumped a small baggie of white powder on top of it. He began to crush it up with a credit card.

"They call him DaVinci because, much like the painter, he works without lines or borders," he said.

I asked him, "How the fuck does that explain what we're doing here?"

"DaVinci is inviting us into the Golden Age."

"The Golden Age of what?"

"The Golden Age of Drug Dealing."

I thought about it for a second. A Mexican guy, with an Asian tattoo, named after an Italian Renaissance painter, was about to usher us into the Golden Age of Drug Dealing?

"We're about to make more money than God," my brother said.

"But DaVinci's Mexican. I thought most Mexicans were Catholics, and we're Jews... so is it Catholic God, or Jewish God?"

Vinny pulled out a hundred-dollar bill, rolled it up, and railed a line off the CD case. He lifted his head.

"Jewish God has a bigger bank account."

13.

On a bright Sunday morning, Vinny picked me up at my house and drove us to New Jersey to visit Sammy in the hospital.

When we arrived at the visitor parking lot, I didn't want to leave the car. Vinny got out of the car first and realized I wasn't moving. I felt sick whenever I visited Sammy. It devastated me. He opened my door, dipped his head into the car, and looked at me. I choked on my words.

"Vinny, it kills me to see him like this."

"I know, kid, but you have to be strong. Not for you, but for him. We're brothers, and do you know what brothers do until the day we die."

"What's that?"

"We love each other."

I dug deep and found my courage. I wiped my tears and buried my sadness.

Vinny was greeted by the nurse, who was familiar with him from his frequent visits. He introduced me to her as we were escorted to Sammy's room. When we reached the door, she said to please let her know if we needed anything. We thanked her and entered.

Vinny walked in before me and was instantly bright and cheerful with Sammy. I was still timid, trying to find my bearings. Sammy could manage to speak a few words, but not many. The trauma from his brain injury left him sounding mumbled and goofy when he spoke. I did my best to force a smile, but I was crushed.

We helped Sammy into a wheelchair, pushed him to the elevator, and headed to the cafeteria for a Mountain Dew and a Three Musketeers bar. He always said it was his favorite candy bar because it represented the three of us. Sammy still had issues with his jaw, so he ate slowly and sipped from a straw. Afterward, Vinny suggested we go outside for some air, so we pushed Sammy to a nearby exit.

The hospital courtyard had a small garden that served as a common area for the long-term residents. Vinny reached inside the pocket of his leather jacket and broke out a perfectly rolled joint. Sammy looked at Vinny, and he said with the biggest smile I'd seen on his face in years.

"Be polite. Pass to the right."

He was still the older brother I'd always known and loved. Vinny took a few puffs and held the joint to my brother's mouth because he still lacked mobility in his arms. Sammy coughed, smiled, and laughed. It was as if nothing had changed between us. At that moment, we were doing what we did best our entire lives. We were living as brothers.

For over an hour, we laughed and reminisced about old times. Eventually, clouds began to pour in. It looked like a summer thunderstorm was coming. We hurried inside before the drizzle turned to a downpour. I held the door as Vinny pushed Sammy back through the lobby towards the elevator.

We returned to Sammy's room and helped him get back into the hospital bed. Sammy groaned from the atrophy in his body as we moved him. It broke my heart to know he was still in so much pain, even after all these years. Vinny took the lead, he wrapped up our visit with good spirits and positive energy.

"Meet me down at the car. I'm going to use the bathroom," Vinny said as he left the room.

It was just the two of us now. Sammy looked at me as the rain pounded on the window pane. I guess the weather was right on time. I told him about my new criminal career path and that no one in our family knew what I was doing except for Vinny.

"Sammy, I've been lost for a long time. I don't know what my future holds, but I want to ensure that you get the best possible care. I don't want you living here. Home is where you belong."

I knew in my heart he would do the same thing for me if I were in that bed. His face conveyed his understanding. He struggled to get his words out.

"Be careful," Sammy said.

"I know I'm not living right, but I ask God every day to watch over me until I find a way to fix this."

I grabbed my brother's hand. Tears hung in my eyes as I spoke.

"I promise I'll get you out of here. I'll do whatever it takes."

I walked toward the elevator and ignored the world around me. My new partnership with DaVinci offered me a level of income that could improve the quality of Sammy's life. After seeing him in that hospital bed, I was more determined than ever to make that happen.

I stepped slowly out of the elevator, but my mind was running full force. I pushed open the hospital doors and walked into the storm that waited outside. Heartache was all I knew, but there were no more tears to cry. The sky was doing it for me.

14.

There are no windows in casinos. The architects leave them out of the design so patrons can gamble without the guilt of witnessing the sunrise after a night of turning cards, tossing dice, and tugging on slot machines. The laws of nature can not be allowed to inform the emotions of the patrons. There can be no parallel between the cycle of life and the cycle of profit.

At three in the morning, my cell phone rang. It was DaVinci.

"Hello."

"I'm in Atlantic City. Come get me," he said.

I inhaled a coffee, got dressed, and headed out. It's a one-hour drive from Philly to Atlantic City. I made it to Caesars Palace in forty-five minutes. I met DaVinci in the lobby of the hotel.

"Have you been drinking?" he asked me.

"No, but I can tell you have."

"Go up to my room, get the bags, load them in the car, and wait for me out front."

I did as he instructed and waited in the car. DaVinci came out of the casino a few moments later and hopped into the back seat.

"Drive the speed limit, and don't stop until we get to the house."

Slow and steady wins the race back to Philly. As I crossed over the Ben Franklin Bridge, my eyes stuck to the mirrors, looking for state troopers as I crossed into Pennsylvania and left New Jersey behind.

I drove up Interstate 95, down the alley, and parked around back. DaVinci told me to bring the bags inside. He drew the blinds and locked the doors.

"Go and grab a bin from the garage."

I assumed we were breaking up some high-end weed, so I closed the blinds and ran out to grab a plastic bin from the garage. DaVinci worked around the clock, but I was exhausted. I wanted to get this done so I could go back to bed. I didn't know it then, but I wouldn't be going to sleep for a while.

I came back inside and placed the bin on the coffee table. DaVinci opened one of the bags. He pulled out a small tightly wrapped pound of weed covered in black duct tape.

"What are we selling, Bibles? What type of weed is this?"

"Get me a knife, and I'll show you."

He cut a slice down the side of the black brick to peel back the plastic.

A glimmering yellowish, white powder gave off a fishy smell. I was star-struck. I felt like a kid on Christmas morning. Snow came drifting down into my living room. Every one of those black bricks was cocaine.

DaVinci poured some on the back of his hand, then pushed the brick towards me.

"Have you ever tried coke?"

"No."

"Try some. You're a growing boy."

I laughed.

"Thanks, but no thanks."

That didn't stop DaVinci from indulging.

We emptied the bricks into the plastic bin, measured them into equal amounts in small glass containers, and placed them in the fridge. It was like the Heineken commercial with a refrigerator full of beer. Only ours was full of cocaine.

That night, when I went to sleep, I brought a sealed black brick up to my room and cuddled it like a teddy bear. However, rest did not come easy. I was up all night long from second-hand exposure to cocaine particles. I didn't realize I could get high from handling cocaine without a mask and gloves. I guess I'd unintentionally taken DaVinci up on his offer after all.

As I hugged that brick of cocaine, my mind raced, imagining how much money I could make. In the presence of that beautiful white powder, I realized how far I'd come from stealing cars. Before I met DaVinci, the most I had ever seen was four and a half ounces of blow. When I thought about the yellow brick road, I never would have imagined it was paved with cocaine. I felt like the coolest motherfucker on earth.

***

DaVinci's lifestyle captivated me. After years without direction, I had found a purpose. It may have been the wrong purpose, but it made me happy to feel valued by someone who could snap their fingers and change my life. DaVinci trusted me with millions of dollars, but it meant nothing compared to knowing that he respected me. I never valued the money as much as I valued his friendship. He gave me an opportunity, and that meant everything to me.

At first, I was overwhelmed by the size and scale of his operation, but he did his best to help me adapt to my new line of work. While driving together from Philadelphia to Chicago, DaVinci gave me his set of seven basic rules for success.

"Listen, learn, and apply," he said.

I sat up like it was the first day of school. Not that I paid attention in class, but you know what I mean. As he spoke, I memorized everything he told me.

Rule number one: *Don't get arrested.*

"It makes you a liability," DaVinci said.

"I closed down all my previous partnerships. I only work with you now," I said.

"Good, because people will step away and disassociate from you if you get arrested. No matter who you are, no one is exempt from this rule while operating. You got it?"

"I got it. What's rule number two?"

Rule number two: *Don't get arrested.*

"This is a dangerous game. They can taste the blood in the water. To remain free, you must deal with only those you can trust. If you find yourself in the open ocean, the sharks will come for you."

Rule number three: *No guns.*

"Never bring a gun to a meeting, ever. If there are guns at a meeting, it's a meeting you are not supposed to be at."

DaVinci explained that the overall picture of crime depicted through music, cinema, and pop culture was unrealistic. Considering the industry we worked in, I found this counterintuitive.

"You might think violence would protect our assets, but it's quite the opposite. Violence doesn't solve problems... it creates them. Look at Kiki," he said.

I had no idea what DaVinci meant by Kiki. In February 1985, an American intelligence officer for the DEA (Drug Enforcement Administration) Enrique "Kiki" Camarena Salazar was kidnapped by drug traffickers hired by Mexican politicians. Kiki was interrogated, tortured, and murdered in Guadalajara, Mexico. DaVinci overestimated my knowledge of his world. Unsure of the reference, I said nothing as he spoke.

"We're not talking local dealer shit. I'm talking about operating on national and international levels. The government allows, or for a better word, tolerates, a certain amount of crime. When people get hurt or murdered, the violence attracts the Feds, and when the Feds come, you will exist no more."

At that time, I associated the Feds with John Gotti, Waco, Texas, and 9/11. I thought they only arrested super criminals. What could they possibly want with someone like me? I thought about what he said. I now know that I was too young to fully digest the magnitude of his following words.

"When you're handed an indictment on a piece of paper with your name on it versus the United States Of America, your life is over."

Rule number four: *Separate the money from the drugs.*

"Never transport money and drugs at the same time. That way, if you violate rules number one and two, you minimize the charges, and will be looking at less time in prison."

The standard protocol for most transactions went like this. Ship the work. Hop on a plane. Attend the meeting. Make the exchange. Count the money, once by hand, once with a money counter. Verify there's no counterfeit currency, and vacuum-seal the cash. Dip the sealed bags of money in alcohol to sterilize them from any lingering drug residue. Stuff the bags into designated stash spots and foam spray them into hidden paneling within cars or large trucks. Seal the paneling shut and check for any aesthetic flaws that could arouse suspicion upon inspection. Set up delivery time and address. Provide the driver with the route. Dispatch. Repeat.

Rule number five: *Never say you have it unless you have it in hand.*

"The fastest way to lose business is when you tell someone to get a large sum of cash together and fail to provide the product. No one, and I mean no one, wants to be sitting around waiting for you with a million dollars in cash."

Listening to DaVinci's rules, I realized they truly were built for success. Competitors down the road approached me to work for them, but I remained loyal to DaVinci every time. That is what separated us from the rest of the animals.

The price of admission to make life-changing money in ten days, not ten years, was my total commitment. We are not talking about landing on free parking type money. We're talking boardwalk, park place, advance to go, all four railroads, and a get-out-of-jail-free card.

Rule number six: *Never rush.*

"When you rush, you're only rushing to one place: prison. If you have an order, no matter how much money there is, do not, and I mean do not rush. Patience is beyond a virtue. It's the difference between freedom or incarceration."

As I became more entwined in the business, DaVinci taught me patience. I thought of all the crimes I got away with based on pure luck. A "fuck it" mentality that had brought me close to being arrested many times.

"Dress well, slick your hair back, wear a suit, and smile. Be precise, be calm. These are significant details in your demeanor—"

"So that's why you asked me if I had tattoos—"

"—The police perpetuate stereotypes of what the bad guy looks like. Pants hanging off your ass, scars, tattoos, gold teeth, etc. This is their criminal."

"So... what's the seventh rule?" I asked.

Rule number seven: *Limit your exposure.*

"High volumes of transactions will make you money, but it's a guaranteed one-way ticket to prison. Every transaction exposes you, exposure increases risk. Reduce your transactions, reduce your risk."

"DaVinci... are you saying that the higher up the food chain we go, the lower our chances of getting arrested become?"

"Correct. In any city, we only supply one guy. Ignore. Irrelevant. Short money. Make moves that matter, life is like chess. Less moves, more money."

***

There was the normal world. A world that adhered to the traditional structure of life in America, one comprised of law-abiding citizens with a mortgage, job, marriage, and kids, but DaVinci opened my eyes to a new world. A world that I had only read about in newspapers or seen in movies. I always knew that it must exist somewhere outside of a Hollywood studio, but the fact that it operated like any other business in America was mind-blowing.

DaVinci introduced me to major plugs all over the country. These plugs are known and referred to as "Big Fish." Once I worked out the logistics with each distributor, I immediately started making sales and setting up future transactions. I learned about supply, demand, wholesale prices, networks, and infrastructure. Pay scales were based on location, delivery, and the quantity of the product. Every order was delivered within seventy-two hours.

My routes were New York, Los Angeles, Chicago, and Houston. Life moved at a thousand miles per hour. I never understood the true scope and scale of the United States until DaVinci had me running all over it. It was at once vast and overwhelming while simultaneously quaint and familiar. I could drive for eight hundred miles across West Texas and exit the interstate, only to find an intersection with a McDonald's, a gas station, and a Motel 6 that looked exactly like an intersection you might find in New Jersey, California, Montana, or Florida.

I moved in and out of major cities undetected by the authorities. I didn't drink alcohol or use drugs. I wore a suit and tie, followed the local laws, and only left the hotel to attend meetings. I carried fake passports and driver's licenses so I could abscond from justice in the event of an unfortunate encounter with law enforcement. Every move was thoroughly calculated to minimize my risk.

I assumed that dirty money funded this whole operation. I was wrong. Most of the money that was invested in our business had nothing to do with selling drugs. Our private investors didn't care where the money came from as long as their returns came in on time. Doctors, lawyers, bankers, you name it, they all wanted in— greed begets immorality. Cash is a language, and no matter where you are in the world, people speak it fluently.

Shortly after I started working with DaVinci, I was introduced to a new client in Philadelphia. He was a high-profile neurosurgeon who worked in one of the local hospitals. Upon our first meeting, he escorted me into a hospital through a back entrance to a private staff room, where we counted the money for his order. He was extremely paranoid throughout the entirety of our transaction, not for fear of getting arrested but because he was concerned about me revealing the nature of our transaction to one of his co-workers. One co-worker in particular.

"Please don't tell your mother," he said while shoving a brick of cocaine into his doctor's bag.

Yes, that's correct. He had worked in the same hospital as my mom for years. They knew each other well, which was none of my business. Who am I to tell a man with a PhD what kind of medicine he should prescribe to his patients?

***

Life for me in Philadelphia would never be the same. DaVinci was a man about town, and I was his right-hand man. Everywhere we went, we were treated like royalty. We lived in sky-high condos, drove luxury cars, and worked on our own time. No experience, object, or desire went unfulfilled.

DaVinci had me under his wing. He treated me like an apprentice, but our relationship extended beyond work. He trusted me unconditionally, and over time, we became best friends.

DaVinci had it all, but he lived an isolated life. The more money and power that he acquired, the more barriers he put up to protect himself. I believe he valued relationships more than anything that money could buy.

***

Delilah's was a steakhouse and gentleman's club that DaVinci would frequent during the day to avoid crowds of people. While it was a strip club, I never saw him buy a lap dance, speak to the dancers, or pay them much mind. He only went for drinks and the occasional steak.

One afternoon, we sat down at a booth for lunch together. The place was empty. A few girls came over to talk with us. They asked us if we wanted a dance. DaVinci handed them some cash and sent them on their way.

"Why don't you ever get a dance?" I asked.

"Out of respect for my wife."

I had worked with him for almost two years and had no idea he was married.

"Does your wife live in Philly?"

"She used to."

I didn't want to overstep my boundaries regarding his personal life, but since we had grown closer, I couldn't contain my curiosity.

"She used to?" I asked.

"I took a trip to Mexico and brought my family with me. I'm the only one who came back."

I wasn't sure if he was serious or not.

"What happened?"

"I learned a hard lesson about the price of doing business. It was a tough pill to swallow. Always protect the people you love."

15.

"You need to come home right now," Lana demanded, panicked.

I was in the middle of a meeting with DaVinci downtown when she called.

"Are you okay? What's going on?" I said.

"Please just come home right now!"

I cut my meeting short and raced home.

I rushed through the door and called out her name. I found Lana in the living room, seated on the couch. The expression on her face conveyed a mixture of confusion, fear, and disappointment. Vacuum-sealed bricks of cash lay on the living room floor amidst scattered pieces of drywall and broken ceiling tiles.

The night that I met Lana at Blue Martini changed the course of my life. I began spending all my free time with her when I wasn't working. She didn't press me about the nature of my work, but I also never told her exactly what I did. I told myself I wasn't lying to Lana, but we both knew I wasn't being honest with her.

Shortly after we started dating, we decided to move in together. I wanted to live in something brand new, but she wanted to feel the history of Philadelphia in our home. We agreed on a chic townhouse built in the 1920s. The building was old, but the interior was fully remodeled— except for the attic.

Our honeymoon phase was short-lived. That night, it all came crashing down... literally. I kept my business dealings outside of our home, but I still had a bad habit of keeping cash inside the house.

Lana had been dancing in the bedroom with huge speakers on full blast. The vibrations from the music must have caused just enough of a rattle in the attic to shake loose the stacks of cash between the insulation and drywall of the ceiling. I must have put too much in one spot because the weight wasn't distributed properly, and it all came crashing down while she listened to her favorite song *Maybe I'm Amazed* by Paul McCartney.

"Babe, it's not what you think," I said as I took a seat next to her on the couch.

As the words came out of my mouth, I noticed for the first time that she still had chunks of drywall stuck in her hair.

"What do you mean it's not what I think? You have a bunch of cash hidden in the ceiling."

At that moment, the only thing I could think about was asbestos.

"Relax," I said while scouring my mind for an excuse.

"Don't tell me to relax. What do you really do, and where did this money come from?"

"Listen... I see loopholes in the system and exploit them. That's all I do, nothing more, nothing less."

"What the hell does that mean?"

She was too smart not to see through the mask that I wore every day. I loved her and trusted her, but I didn't want to reveal myself to her in a different light. I only wanted Lana to see the good side of me.

"I want you to stop," she said.

"It's not that easy. It's complicated."

"Like how? Explain it to me then."

"I can't."

"Try."

"I made a promise to someone, and I have to keep it. I need a certain amount of money to make that happen."

"Isn't this enough money?" Lana said as she looked at the massive pile of cash on the floor. "Please, I love you. I need to know what's going on. Just tell me, I can accept whatever it is."

I took a deep breath and exhaled slowly.

"I'm only doing this until I raise enough money to get my brother home and out of the hospital."

"Your brother? I don't understand."

Although I trusted Lana, I kept the relationship dynamics of my family a secret. My life was a mess, but I did my best to keep my side of the street clean. I didn't want my problems to ever become hers.

"As I said, it's complicated. Trust me. Please just trust me, Lana. Can you do that ?"

"I can. Please don't lie to me."

"I won't. I love you, Lana. Now, can you please get in the shower?"

That experience brought us closer together. After the shower, we lay in bed and talked. I didn't want to share the entire truth about my work, but I couldn't help but offer some details to help ease her concerns.

Lana treated me better than anyone I had ever known, and she accepted me for who I was. She let me share a side of myself with her that I had never shared with anyone before. My laugh, why I smile, and what makes me cry. I shared my inner child with her, my love, and the thing I guarded most: my heart.

16.

The outside of the club was discreet. *District* written in red was the only signage above the entrance that was nothing more than an oxblood velvet drape. All it took to pull back the curtain was a brief walk of shame down a dusty street.

Mariachi music invaded my thoughts. Female silhouettes glided down from the ceiling on golden poles covered in neon lights and cigarette smoke. Antonio and I pushed through the crowd. Two chairs that sat center stage had our names on them. We needed to kill time as we waited for Big Fish's associates to arrive.

DaVinci refused to ever step foot in Mexico again. He sent me to represent him and delegate future shipments coming North. Antonio worked for DaVinci in New York and was the epitome of every New Yorker I had ever met. Cunning, dangerous, and talked out of the side of his mouth. I considered him an acquaintance. His eyes trailed after topless women in cowboy boots.

"Have you met *Big Fish?*" Antonio shouted over the music.

"No."

A random cowgirl grabbed his cash, blew a kiss, and returned to the stage.

"Drinks, more drinks," Antonio shouted as he stood up to dance.

I clocked two guys wearing Versace shades as soon as they entered. Dressed in all black, the associates of Big Fish had arrived. I stood and shook their hands. They introduced themselves, but I couldn't hear their names. I called them Tito and Chino. Tito gestured a circling finger in the air toward the bartender.

"*Cervezas!*"

The waitress dropped a bucket of beer on the table. Tito whispered to the waitress and slid her some cash. He raised his beer to toast the song he'd requested.

"*Por las mala' o por las buenas.*"

We clinked bottles and drank.

After a few more clubs and a lot more alcohol, Tito and Chino drove us to meet Big Fish.

When we arrived, I finally understood why they called him Big Fish. He must have been three hundred pounds and almost seven feet tall. Oddly enough, his nickname had nothing to do with his physical stature but rather the amount of product he controlled and distributed.

"*¿Cómo estás, Pinche gringos?*" Big Fish exclaimed, arms wide open.

Big Fish was much friendlier than I had anticipated. He shook Antonio's hand but ignored my handshake as an introduction and pulled me in for a hug.

"DaVinci says you're his right-hand man," he said as I got a face full of armpit.

"That's right," I managed.

A three-car heavily guarded convoy pulled into the driveway. Two black SUVs sandwiched a white Mercedes like an Oreo in the middle.

"That's a W100," I said.

"Impressive gringo. How would someone so young know such an automobile?"

"Not at your level, but I've collected a few cars here and there," I shrugged.

"You are definitely an American."

The convoy kicked up a trail of dust off the red rocks onto the red taillights. Red on red, rust on blood. We drove deep into the foothills of the dark mountains that loomed ahead. Adrenaline pumped through my veins as we traveled in style like rich oil Sheikhs. True, these guys did gain their wealth from the ground, but the big difference was they didn't dress in white, they sold it. I lost all sense of direction as we passed by a gate that cordoned off a small road that led to a plateau surrounded by peaks.

I stepped out to a barren wasteland illuminated only by a full moon that sat like a parrot on the mountain's shoulder. Five of us sat down at a single table cemented into the ground. *Cervezas* and tacos were brought out by a woman whose personal appearance resembled her workplace surroundings. She welcomed us as a mother does, then disappeared into the taco stand. We toasted to family.

"How much work do you move for DaVinci and what other product can you handle?" Big Fish inquired.

I knew where this conversation was headed.

"*No más DaVinci*. Cut the middleman. Represent me in your cities."

I attempted to speak up for us, but Antonio's impulsive nature beat me to it.

"I can handle anything you want to send."

"*Bueno,*" Big Fish said, "And you? I offer wealth, yet you hesitate."

His accent was thick and heavy. From the tone of his voice, I felt pessured to agree. Not sure how to decline, I paused.

"I work for DaVinci."

"My money's not green?" Big Fish's expression shifted.

"I'll take the offer," Antonio said.

Big Fish looked to Antonio, then back to me.

"My offer is now *gringo*."

"While I appreciate the offer, DaVinci is a brother to me."

"He was right," Big Fish muttered.

His hand came up from under the table with a large revolver. I saw bullet tips in the chamber.

"This is the benefit of disloyalty," Big Fish said.

The associates chimed in. They spoke with a frightening calm. "Leave him. Just leave homie here. We'll take care of it. Leave him."

I paused mid-bite of my taco. The desert was suddenly cold. If you have never been this close to death, it's difficult to explain the feeling that washes over you. Fear is followed by acceptance. Stillness. I was a ceramic dog, frozen in the Mexican night.

Is this how it ends?

The terrain was flat, barren, and now resembled a graveyard more than a desert. There was nowhere to run. The tacos smelled like death.

Big Fish took out his phone, dialed, and leaned back in his chair. He held the phone to his ear and waited. The conversation was brief.

"Both of them?"

He paused. The inaudible voice on the phone continued. I heard the grit of metal friction as Big Fish rotated the gun toward Antonio. He glanced at me.

"Don't worry, little homie, you're good, but your homeboy isn't."

My eyes fixed on the gun. A .357 Magnum. The hair trigger was cocked back to fire.

"Who's it gonna be?" Big Fish turned towards me.

I surveyed the table.

"I know this might be a bad time, but is he going to eat that?" The Big Fish and his associates laughed.

"In all seriousness, fellas, you can split the check four ways."

***

Windows down, music up, and wind whipping through the cabin of the car, I blazed up the California Interstate. I couldn't get away from Mexico fast enough. The next phase of this job was to get the product back to Philadelphia.

Typically, a motorcade of cars from different states accompanied shipments headed Northeast. We used scanners to listen for the authorities and Nextel phones to communicate as we drove. The use of several cars helped disguise and protect the primary vehicle carrying the load. We are not talking about a few cop stickers and soccer mom logos on the bumper. We hired drivers who fit the profile of what we wanted to portray, the average American family.

When I made this run, however, I had no motorcade, and the term for this insane dash across America is called *Cowboying*. Cowboying meant you head to the middle of nowhere, pick up work, fill the car, and when I say to fill the car, I mean pack it to the brim like you're going on vacation. Then you hit the gas, giddy up, and *go*.

Red Bull and the promise of a hundred-thousand-dollar paycheck kept me awake through the lengthy drive. That, and the thought of how much time in prison I was going to be serving if I fell asleep at the wheel. Have I danced with the devil in the pale moonlight? No, but I've eaten tacos with Mexicans in the middle of fucking nowhere.

I made my way east early Friday morning before sunrise and ripped across America as Saturday stretched into Sunday. Before I knew it, I was a few states away from Pennsylvania. The hand on the clock had just passed midnight about an hour before I crossed into Indiana. Gusts of wind started to pick up, unlike anything I had experienced before. I sat up straight as rocks and dust began to hit the windows. This storm had my undivided attention. I had no idea about the forecast and couldn't get a signal on the AM radio. The view through my windshield was a cloud of apocalyptic dust. Wind pummeled the car so fiercely that I felt it shift on all four tires as it slid from side to side. The faster I drove, the more Mother Nature bullied the car across the highway.

I finally heard a voice come across the static of my radio as I flipped frantically through my stations for a sign from God. A voice came across the radio and exclaimed loudly in a midwestern drawl.

Mattresses, mattresses, mattresses! Bouncy mattresses! Softy mattresses! Firm mattresses! Slightly used mattresses! Or new! We got—

I spun the dial again. Just as I did, a cluster of wire fencing flew across the highway and nearly hit my car.

"Jesus Christ!" I yelled.

—*is your savior,* shouted the radio back at me through a burst of static. The winds roared even louder.

Have you considered your actions today? Have you repented for your sins?

These weren't the words I wanted to hear at that exact moment. Why was I here? How did I end up in the middle of a fucking tornado? While you may think Indiana is full of rednecks, I can assure you that I was the only hillbilly dumb enough to drive through that storm.

Debris flew past my windshield, and the visibility was so bad that I could only make out a small piece of road in front of me. There was nowhere to run or hide.

Stopping the car and waiting out the storm wouldn't save me. I had no other choice. I had to get out of there as fast as possible. I white-knuckled the wheel and pressed on through the storm at a hundred miles per hour.

God, go with me.

I began to pray, but as a Jew who failed out of a Catholic school, I struggled to find the proper words.

"Our Mother... who art in heaven... Hollywood be thy bread... forgive our trespassing as the priest did trespass against us... forgive my sins, or at least this one?"

My poor attempt at performing the sign of the cross over my forehead and chest made me decide to switch gears. I continued with reciting whatever I could remember from the Torah.

"Barukh ata Adonai Eloheinu... Shaquille kugel O'Neal, Kareem matzoh ball Abdul-Jabbar, Hakeem lox on a bagel Olajuwon, Melech ha'olam, Kobe latkes Bryant."

Realizing my state of panic had me either ordering at a Jewish deli or reciting my favorite NBA players, I felt it best to quit while I was ahead.

By the grace of God, I made it out of that tornado alive with my vehicle and the million dollars of product still intact. I tuned in to the radio. That storm was very real, and the damage was devastating.

The tornado touched down near the Indiana/Kentucky border and then crossed the Ohio River into Indiana. It lasted about twenty minutes and was the deadliest tornado to hit Indiana in the past few decades. Twenty-two people died, one hundred and fifty people were injured, hundreds of homes were destroyed, and one young man from Philadelphia passed through it unscathed with a car full of cocaine.

17.

Every time I said goodbye to Lana, I died a little inside. We had grown closer than ever since the asbestos incident. If I wasn't working, I was with her. So, it was only natural that she introduced me to her family. She was a good woman from a good home, and I was a man who came from a broken one. When she asked about my family, I'd change the subject. Lana knew I had a family, but much like my life of crime, I kept them separate because I understood the nature of our relationship.

We were two kids falling in love, but I feared how this story would end. I lied to myself, swearing I would make it right. I wanted to protect this beautiful thing I had. She was the only thing that brought me joy. It was the first time in my life that a woman had told me she loved me. When she first said it, I didn't say it back. Not because I didn't love her but because I was afraid that I might lose her love one day. In the back of my mind, I was acutely aware that because of my lifestyle, something terrible could happen to me. I wanted her to remember me at my best. The hard truth about my best is that my best could get me killed or sent to prison.

One evening, we were home together watching a movie when she lifted her head from my chest and looked at me. I wrapped her in my arms and squeezed her every time she tried to get up. She giggled with delight because she knew the key to unlocking my arms was a kiss. Young lust. We tore each other's clothes off.

Moments later, we were in the bedroom. Lana lay on top of me. She looked like every song and movie about love I had ever known. We were so distracted that neither of us noticed what was happening.

I looked down and saw blood. It wasn't just a little bit of blood from normal menstruation. She was bleeding everywhere. Her face went blank. She was in a state of shock. I ran to the bathroom and grabbed a towel.

When I came back, she was sobbing uncontrollably. I cleaned her off, dressed her, and wrapped her in a blanket. I threw on some sweatpants, grabbed her in my arms, and carried her to the car. I saw panic in her eyes as I loaded her into the back seat.

The hospital was twenty minutes from our home. I was already flying down Market Street. I looked into the backseat and saw her eyes fluttering. Lana was in severe pain and close to losing consciousness. I slammed my foot down on the gas.

A giant red sign jumped out in front of me. The words emergency room loomed overhead. I parked, hopped out, and grabbed her from the back seat. I left my door open, with the engine still running, and ran inside.

"Help! She needs help! Help me, please!"

She was limp in my arms. The nurses rushed around the counter and helped me place her on a gurney. I put her down as gently as I could.

"We got it from here, sir," one of the nurses said.

I tried to follow them, but they stopped me. I stood there helplessly. I had never felt so alone. I looked down at my arms. They were covered in blood.

I sat down in the waiting room chair. My head was heavy in my hands. I thought back over the past few days. Throughout the week, Lana had been suffering from stomach pains that she assumed were signs that her menstrual cycle was coming.

I waited through the night, nodding in and out of sleep. The walls, the chairs, the smells, coffee, the vending machine meals, and the rooms full of sad people were all so familiar. I thought about my brother and the suffering he had to endure, living in a place like this.

Over and over, I asked for a status update on Lana. The nurse repeated herself.

"The doctor will come to see you when they have an answer. Please be patient."

Somewhere in the haze of stress and exhaustion, I heard a voice.

"Excuse me, the doctor is requesting to speak with you."

I followed the nurse through double doors to where the doctor waited for me. This small room gave off the negative ambiance of bad news and trauma. *Please don't be true.*

"Are you Lana's boyfriend?" the doctor asked.

"Yes. Is she okay?"

"Please have a seat."

Not again, not again. I can't do this twice.

"She's stable and out of surgery."

"Surgery? What surgery?"

"Unfortunately, we can't discuss that with you. Only she can."

"Why not? I'm her boyfriend!"

"I'm sorry, but it's hospital policy. You're not an immediate family member to the patient."

"Can I see her?"

"Yes, but she's a bit out of it. Please be brief. She needs to rest."

Lana was on her side with her back toward me when I entered the room. The beeping of the monitors. The clamor of the hospital. The echoes in the hallways. This time, they were louder than ever.

I walked around the side of the bed to lean down and kiss her. She reached up and hugged me tight. Her tears rolled down my neck. She didn't make a sound. I pulled up a chair alongside the bed and sat down. Her face was pale, and her tears had stopped, though I could still feel them on my neck.

"I had an ectopic pregnancy. In my heart, I know it was a little girl."

So many things passed through my mind at that moment. We wanted a baby; she had been trying to get pregnant, and our dream was to start a family together. I never imagined something like this could happen. I was a dad? I was crushed. With no time to ponder the thought, I suppressed my daydream. Lana needed me here now, in the moment.

"They removed one of my ovaries. The doctor said I had some complications."

"What does that mean, Lana?"

She closed her eyes. She sobbed uncontrollably.

"The doctor said most likely, I won't be able to have children, I'm broken. No one will ever want me."

Love is an unconditional term for me. There is no limit. None. She was my partner, and I would never abandon someone I love. She had my heart, and she had it forever.

"I love you, Lana. We'll find a way, no matter what it takes."

18.

"Pick me up in twenty minutes. Come in one of *your cars*," DaVinci said and hung up the phone.

Your cars meant DaVinci wanted me to drive an untraceable vehicle. We were about to do something illegal. I grabbed the car keys, cash, and a fake ID.

It was early afternoon, and the sun was blazing. Heat waves fumed off the pavement. I pulled the car up in front of DaVinci's high-rise condo downtown and waited. When I saw him walk out, I jumped out and opened the rear door.

We hit the road. A glance in the rearview mirror told me he was in a shitty mood. DaVinci partied because he lived that life, but I didn't. I often worked long hours on short sleep but kept a positive attitude. Sometimes, the stress of working for DaVinci on-call got on my nerves.

"Rough night?" I asked sarcastically.

He didn't look up from his phone.

"Head to the stash house."

"What's the plan here, DaVinci?"

He was already on a call. He leaned his mouth briefly away from the phone.

"Drive."

DaVinci made multiple phone calls along the way, switching between several phones as he did so. I arrived at our destination, a small warehouse on the edge of Northeast Philly. He jumped out as soon as I parked.

"Wait here."

The heat was oppressive. I grew irritated as I sat and watched the minutes tick by on the clock. I waited for thirty minutes before DaVinci came outside. He hopped back in the car with a maroon alligator-skin duffle bag.

"Cottman and the Boulevard."

"No problem," I replied.

It would take forty-five minutes to get to the Boulevard at this time of day. The traffic was a nightmare. DaVinci told me to take a specific route that he thought would be faster. The Roosevelt Mall and a smoke shop called Artifax were down there. The area was always swarming with cops. I didn't understand the urgency and I knew a better route, but DaVinci was set in his ways.

Ah, the choices we make in life. DaVinci was rarely hands-on in conducting business and paid people like me to take care of these things for him. He seldom made a personal appearance for anyone.

"*Qué pasó*," came from the back seat.

"Traffic, DaVinci, traffic."

"Let's go, get around it. Hurry up. I've got shit to do."

DaVinci leaned forward and gave me instructions.

"Drop me off, dump these phones, buy more, and get ready to leave. We have a flight to catch later. Turn left onto Cottman."

"We can't turn here," I said.

He looked through the windows and then behind us.

"Just do it."

I knew better, especially in a stolen car. I turned left onto Cottman Avenue. My eyes were in my rearview mirror. We made it only a few hundred feet before I watched a police car zip around the same turn we had just taken. I knew in my gut what was about to happen. I waited for it. The cop hit the lights.

"Lace-up, homie. It's go time!" I yelled.

DaVinci looked back at the flashing lights behind us.

He let out a long string of curses, most of which were in Spanish. The only word I understood was *fuck*.

I accelerated slowly to open up a little more distance between us and the police.

"What's in the bag?" I shouted.

"Two things you never keep together, and a lifetime behind bars!"

"Fuck me!" I said.

DaVinci looked back at the police, and then at me. Our eyes locked in the rearview mirror. For the first time since I met him, he seemed unsure of himself.

Without a second thought, I reached back and said, "Here, take my phone. This one's clean."

I turned into an alleyway and acted like I was pulling over to cooperate with the police. The car's license plate was a copy of a legitimate one, so we had a little time before the police discovered that we had violated rule number four.

Separate the money from the drugs.

I turned around and looked at DaVinci.

"I'll lead the police away. They are coming after me since I'm the driver. When I get us far enough away from them, I'll slam the car into park, and we'll run."

"Are you fucking kidding?"

"— you go right, and I'll go left. Dump whatever the fuck is in that bag."

I reached through the steering column with my left arm, ready to kill the ignition. My right hand was on the shifter.

"Does it look like I'm fucking kidding?"

I looked in my sideview mirror and watched the cop step out of his car. He was tall and overweight. I felt my odds of getting away increase when I saw him. As he approached our vehicle, he read off my license plate into his radio. As soon as he arrived at the driver's side door, I punched it and put the pedal to the floor. I opened up some distance between us before he even got back into his police cruiser.

When I made it to the end of the alley, I locked the tires, skidded, and slammed the gear shifter into park. I pulled the key out of the ignition so fast that the transmission didn't register that I'd killed the engine.

I threw the driver's side door open, jumped out, and sprinted for a breakthrough in the alleyway. DaVinci jumped out simultaneously and ran right. I looked over my shoulder and saw the car lurching forward. The engine was choking for life. I heard it crash into a dumpster. The cadence of the bang was different, and the size of the dent was different, but I couldn't help but think of Greg. I wondered if he had been keeping up with his blood pressure medication.

I jumped over two high fences and chucked the keys into a sewer drain next to a line of parked cars. I broke into a full sprint toward Roosevelt Boulevard. I made it six blocks before I came across a man sitting on his steps outside his house. I heard sirens in the distance. Time was running out. I ran up to the man and pulled a wad of cash out of my pocket.

"This is five grand," I said, holding the cash in front of his face. "It's all yours if you let me sit in your living room for one hour."

He looked at the stack of cash in my hand and then back to my face. I was breathing heavily. Perhaps a little too aggressively, I said, "It's your lucky day, my man. Take the money!"

He screamed for help and scrambled up the steps and into the house, slamming the door behind him. The Boulevard was wide open with nowhere to hide. I was in the wrong place at the right time. I stood in the middle of the intersection, hands in plain sight. A dozen police cars came screeching in from every direction.

Cops, guns, and verbal commands encircled me. The officer closest was about five feet away, his firearm trained on the center mass of my torso. I was a black silhouette on a white background at the police shooting range.

"On the fucking ground! You piece of shit motherfucker! Get on the fucking ground!"

"I'm not lying down on that nasty pavement," I calmly said.

"Now, asshole!"

I decided to compromise, so I knelt. The cops rushed in and forced my arms behind my back. They cuffed my wrists with two rolls of shiny nickels.

"Why'd you run?" the officer asked.

"Run? I don't know what you're talking about. I was out for a jog. Can't you see I'm—"

A blow to the back of my head stopped me from finishing my sentence. Without my hands to prevent myself from falling forward, my face hit the ground. I should've known I was destined to end up on that nasty pavement anyway. All I could think about at that moment was that I hoped DaVinci had gotten away.

They brought me back to the car where I had left it in the alleyway.

"Tell us where the car keys are! Where the fuck did your buddy run off to?" one cop asked.

"Don't worry. We're gonna find him," another cop yelled.

I said nothing. They pulled the knot of cash and fake driver's license out of my pocket.

"We got him!"

Got who?

An officer read the name on the license with the enthusiasm of a football coach as he held it up next to my face.

"Nick, we got your ass!" he exclaimed.

There were high-fives and handshakes all around as they celebrated my arrest. The police were about to book me under a fake ID. I tried not to laugh. The minor crime I committed was the biggest bust of their careers. Little did they know that by the time the ink dried on my bail receipt, I'd be gone, and they'd be chasing a ghost.

It was a shitty ride to the 15th District, but I was curious to see if I could make it in and out of the system under a fake name. If I wanted any shot at pulling this off, it would be best to go with the silent approach.

The paddy wagon pulled up to the intake entrance of the police station. The officer opened a battered, mustard-colored steel door and walked me inside. The ambiance matched the prisoner I could see sitting on the toilet through the metal bars of a jail cell. What a dump.

They brought me to the intake area for fingerprinting and a mug shot. The officer asked me for my name, to which I replied, "Okay." He ignored my response and wrote down the name on the fake ID. Who was I to try and stop this outstanding civil servant from doing his job? I went with it. I was told to stand in front of the height chart. Smile. *Click*!

The arrest didn't bother me. What upset me was not knowing if DaVinci had gotten away, and how Lana was going to react to my disappearance.

After three long days in a disgusting cell, I was called for my bail hearing. There was a video camera, a small chair, and a desk for remote communication. The plan was to make no eye contact, avoid looking up at the camera, and limit my responses to as few words as possible. The judge came on screen and started with the usual questions.

"State your name."

"Nick Whottin."

I held my breath while I waited to see if my fake name would pass inspection. The questions continued.

"Address?"

I exhaled. The fake ID worked. I gave them the address on the ID. Next, the judge asked for a few details I wasn't prepared for.

"Have you been arrested before?"

Unsure about the background of whose identity I was using, I took an optimistic approach.

"No, Your Honor."

"How many siblings do you have?"

I responded like I signed up for a charity event.

"Yeah, ah, put me down for a few of those."

Lie after lie. Somehow, they believed it all. The only person who couldn't believe it was me.

"Bail is set at ten thousand dollars," the judge said.

The prosecutor interjected, "Your Honor, Mr. Whottin had five thousand dollars cash on him at the time of his arrest."

The judge, with no delay, responded, "Fifty thousand. Next case."

I returned to my holding cell and waited to see if they would catch me in the act of breaking the law while behind bars, for breaking the law. The fake identity was holding up. A few hours passed before an officer strolled down the hall and called out for me.

"Whottin, where you at? You made bail."

I extended one hand through the bars with two fingers in the air as if summoning a waiter for the bill, and said, "Check, please!"

Pennsylvania is a commonwealth law state, so I needed to pay ten percent of the price of the bond to be released. I still had the five thousand on me, so I paid the bond on the spot.

Straight outta pocket.

The police weren't happy I was getting off lightly and were more than willing to let me know how they felt about it. I was thrown up against the wall and searched one last time in the hopes that they would find drugs on me to prevent me from leaving. I stared them in the eyes with every hundred I laid on the desk as I counted all the things they hated about their miserable lives in the voice of Count von Count from *Sesame Street*.

"One... ex-wife! Ah, Ah, Ah."

"Two... ungrateful kids! Ah, Ah, Ah."

"Three... extra shifts to pay for college! Ah, Ah, Ah."

Once I finished counting out the money, they pointed to the exit and hit me with a barrage of compliments.

"Get the fuck out." "See ya soon asshole." "You piece of shit." "Take it on the arches, pal." "We'll be waiting for you." "Don't let me see you out there." And the list goes on.

I balled up the paperwork and chucked it in the trash before hitting the parking lot. I stepped out into that sweet summer breeze and evaporated into the Philadelphia cityscape.

19.

Weeks passed, and I heard nothing from DaVinci. We had never discussed what to do under those circumstances. DaVinci was never supposed to allow himself to be in that situation in the first place. He broke his own rules that day and put us both in jeopardy. My mind was all over the place.

I had to find DaVinci.

I called the phone I gave him. Nothing. I called all the local districts. Nothing. I called our mutual contacts. Nothing. I tried to locate him in the system. Nothing. DaVinci had vanished. Paranoia took hold of me. I began to think the worst.

One night, as the summer was coming to a close, I lay in bed, unable to sleep. I walked to the pretzel factory at four o'clock in the morning.

"Yo cuz we just made 'em' fresh," the guy behind the counter said as he handed me the pretzel.

I heard a voice behind me.

"Put some mustard on it."

I turned around and saw DaVinci. He was dressed in a black suit.

Had he been there the whole time?

He extended his hand to shake mine as if nothing had happened.

"Take me for a drive."

Due to the nature of future events, I won't disclose exactly where we went, but it was a place I will never forget.

The night faded, and the dawn rolled in. We drove for at least two hours. This was the first and only time I'd ever felt uncomfortable with DaVinci sitting behind me.

How well did I know this guy? How well did my brother know him? If it were anyone else I would never volunteer to put myself in a position like this. Had my desire for money obstructed my instincts for self-preservation?

He said nothing on the ride. The only time he spoke was when he gave me directions.

We pulled off the highway into a wooded area. The sun had just begun to rise. DaVinci directed me to the corner of a dirty parking lot. He opened his door and stepped out of the car.

"Let's take a walk."

Who goes hiking in a suit?

When we made it to the entrance of the trailhead, he stepped aside, extended his arm, and gestured for me to walk in front of him.

I'm glad I wore my new shoes. At least I'll look nice at my funeral.

I took his suggestion and began to walk. In my mind, I contemplated the potential outcomes of this stroll in the woods.

How did I get here? I did what I thought was best for both of us that day.

The trail wound and wound as we climbed higher and higher. At last, we reached the peak of the trailhead. I looked down below me and saw what appeared to be a small lagoon. We walked down to the lagoon and then ascended a small hidden pathway that spiraled upward behind the waterfall.

We stood together at the edge of the waterfall.

I don't know why, but I'm not afraid anymore.

DaVinci removed his jacket and rolled up his sleeve. He pointed at the koi fish tattoo on his arm and gestured toward the water below us.

"The strongest koi fish is the one that swims up the waterfall and reaches the top."

This is not what I was expecting him to say at that moment. DaVinci continued.

"I know why you did what you did—"

"DaVinci—"

"—I was sloppy and arrogant. I'll never put you in that position again. Don't worry about your legal case. I'll get it dropped. You saved my life that day."

I was dumbfounded.

"This tattoo was given to me as a reminder of the oath I gave to the men around me. It was upstream from there, and only death could stop me. One day, you will become that koi fish."

He rotated his arm to show me the entire tattoo.

"It was the first time I made a million dollars."

DaVinci rolled his sleeve down, buttoned his cuff, and put his jacket back on.

"What do you desire in this life?" he asked.

There was only one correct response to this question, and it would take me to hell and back and half of a lifetime to find the answer.

"I want to be remembered with the legacy of a good man."

The truth was that I felt worthless and needed money, so I told him what I thought he wanted to hear. DaVinci was speaking of folklore, and the mythos in my life had only just begun to unfold.

"Your loyalty is that of a brother. You are beyond your years. I trust no one outside my family, but because of what you did, I know you would die to protect me."

He extended his hand toward me. I shook it.

"You must pass through darkness and pain to find your inner truth. We are brothers now, I trust you with my life," he said.

We made our way back down the path toward the car. "How did you find this place?" I asked.

DaVinci raised his arm in front of me to stop us in our tracks. He turned and looked at me.

"Water is the source of life. You can always find your peace in the waterfall."

20.

Work returned to usual, and before I knew it summer had passed as the rains returned to Philadelphia. DaVinci walked into my house unannounced and laid a duffle bag full of cash on the table.

"I need you to handle this."

I glanced at the duffle bag.

"How long?"

He was almost back out the door before I had even finished my reply.

"Stash it for me. I'll call you."

"Wait," I said.

DaVinci paused in the doorway.

"When are you coming back?"

"I have things to handle. Wait for my call"

I moved fast, DaVinci moved faster. We had several unspoken

arrangements, but the magnitude of responsibility he placed on me with his cash is not one that I can say I always enjoyed. There must have been a million dollars in the bag. I counted the money to know exactly how much I was responsible for. Sure enough, it was a million dollars.

A week later, DaVinci called me.

"Bring my duffle bag."

"It's at the stash house buried in the backyard. I'll need an hour," I said.

"Dig it up, and meet me at the lunch spot." He hung up.

An hour later DaVinci was out front of Delilah's waiting for me. He jumped in the car and looked like he hadn't slept in a week.

"You good?" I asked.

He looked at me with wild eyes.

"Drive."

"Drive where?"

He leaned his seat back, placed his hat over his face, and stated one word.

"Vegas."

***

Colorful lights, drunks, hookers, and gamblers lined the street as we drove down the Las Vegas strip. We booked two rooms at the newly opened Wynn Casino and Hotel.

When we got upstairs, I looked around my room for the best place to stash the money. The dresser was the best spot, so I flipped it over and secured the money underneath it. DaVinci and I were scheduled to meet one of his main suppliers from Texas at the Hard Rock Casino early the next morning.

We headed to the bar in the lobby for a nightcap. I ordered a Johnny Walker neat. DaVinci had a Corona with a slice of orange. We discussed our plans for the following day. I didn't know his Texas plug, but DaVinci assured me they would handle most of the business. DaVinci would negotiate terms with them for a working arrangement in Philly. My job was to keep track of the money. He trusted no one, so only when the terms for territory and distribution were agreed upon, would I bring in the cash.

We left the bar and went back up to the hotel room. DaVinci was buzzing with energy, and ready to gamble. I was exhausted from driving and wanted to rest. Nonetheless, I was on edge because of the sheer volume of cash in the hotel room. He grabbed his things and headed for the door.

"Get some rest," he said, "you have a long journey ahead of you."

***

Sunlight broke through the blinds of the hotel room. My head was pounding, but this wasn't a hangover. I only had one drink the night before. The stress was fucking with me. The neon red numbers on the bedside clock drew my attention. Eight a.m. seared my vision. It was eerily quiet in the room. I assumed DaVinci was still out gambling. I called his phone. No answer.

Give him some time. He's never late.

I ordered breakfast, showered, and got ready for the meeting. I called him again. No answer. It was coming down to the wire. I sat in the room, money packed, and ready to go. The silence grew louder. I flipped on the TV to calm my nerves. Horse racing, of course, Las Vegas. I picked up the phone and called again. No answer. Paranoia flooded me. A knock on the door defused my thoughts. DaVinci was right on time.

I picked up the duffle bag and opened the hotel room door. A tiny woman stood next to a cart stacked full of fresh towels.

"Toalla, you need the toalla?"

I looked at the stack of towels in her hand.

"No thanks," I said and shut the door.

What the fuck is going on here?

I had no idea what to do next. I sat there for another hour. No DaVinci.

I flipped the dresser over, stashed the money underneath it, and put everything back in its original place. I crept over and peered through the peephole. I put my ear to the crack of the door and listened for suspicious sounds. All quiet.

I opened the door and popped my head into the hallway. I looked back and forth, but nothing in either direction. I closed the door.

Should I stay or should I go? If I leave and something happens to the money, I'm fucked. If I can't find DaVinci, I'm fucked. If DaVinci was busted, this might be the one shot to get the money out of here... if I get out of here.

I have to get out of here.

I hung the *Do Not Disturb* sign on the handle, closed the door, and checked to ensure that it was locked.

I headed toward the elevator. I had visions of law enforcement surrounding me, throwing me to the ground, and putting a gun to my head. Wouldn't have been the first time. I stepped into the elevator and pressed the button for the ground level.

The elevator doors opened to a sea of bodies on the casino floor. Bright lights and loud noises cascaded over me. I maneuvered through rows of sad souls and slot machines toward the high roller's table. No face escaped my field of vision as I scanned them all on the way.

I have to find DaVinci.

I circled the empty high-stakes tables, just pit bosses, dealers, and shattered dreams. The thought of the unattended cash in my hotel room made me anxious. I quickened my pace. I hurried past the lobby bar and stopped near the Ferrari showroom at the front of the casino. No sign of DaVinci.

Someone is following me.

I stopped and looked around in every direction. I studied the people around me, but I saw no one suspicious. Still, I couldn't shake the feeling that someone was watching me.

I made my way back to the lobby. The front desk concierge was alone. It was the same clerk from the day before.

"Good morning, sir. How can I help you today?"

"I checked in yesterday. Do you remember me?"

"Yes, how can I help you?"

"Do you remember the Mexican guy that checked in with me? Have you seen him by any chance?"

"I'm sorry, sir, but I thought you checked in alone."

"No... I checked in with a friend. Didn't you see him?"

"What's your room number, please?"

His hands flurried and clicked across a keyboard behind the computer.

"It says here one room, one adult."

I couldn't think of anything to say, so I turned and walked away.

What the fuck is going on here?

I spotted a security guard across the lobby and pulled him aside to speak to him. I tried to keep my voice as low as possible.

"Excuse me. I was wondering if the casino could check the surveillance cameras to help me locate someone."

"Is something wrong, sir?"

"No, nothings wrong. I came to meet my friend for lunch but haven't been able to locate him. Just a little strange, that's all."

"Have you tried the front desk?"

"Yes, I have."

"I'm sorry, but we don't share security footage unless a crime has been committed. You can file a missing person report with the local police."

A bead of sweat trickled down my forehead.

"That's okay. I'll figure it out."

I have to get out of this hotel.

I returned to the elevator and began plotting my escape from the casino. The doors opened. I stepped into the hallway and looked towards my hotel room door. That fucking cart with white towels was outside of my room. My heart sank.

The money.

"No! No! I told you I didn't want that!" I screamed at her as I sprinted down the corridor to my hotel door.

I was mid-rant when I realized my mistake. She wasn't in my room. She was in the room across the hall. My paranoia had gotten the best of me. I handed her a wad of cash and apologized. It was definitely time to check out.

When I walked through the lobby, I felt like the entire population of Las Vegas, Nevada, had X-ray vision. All eyes were on the bag in my hand. I crossed the air- conditioned gambling floor and stepped out into the heat of the Las Vegas strip.

***

I had no choice but to return to Philadelphia by myself. I called every hospital and jail in Nevada to see if anyone matched DaVinci's description, but I came up with nothing. I felt like a part of me was missing. Yesterday, I worked in a familiar world, but I now lived in the unknown.

When I arrived home, I kept peaking out the blinds at my car in the driveway that had a million dollars of DaVinci's money in the trunk. I half expected him to call at any moment, but in my heart, I knew he wouldn't.

DaVinci lived in a secure building downtown. I knew I couldn't walk through the front door, so I did what anyone would do… I ordered a pizza.

Mike answered, "Hello."

"I need a solid, my guy."

"Where the hell have you been?"

"No time to explain, but when I call you in thirty minutes, stay on the phone and ignore everything I say."

"Say no more," Mike said.

I called Enzo's Pizza and placed an order for delivery so they would print a slip with DaVinci's address on it. Five minutes later I called back and switched the order from delivery to pick up. I went to Enzos, picked up the pizza, and grabbed a cab to DaVinci's condo downtown.

I walked into the lobby and approached the front desk. The clerk asked me for the condominium number. I pointed to the address on the receipt attached to the pizza box and spoke with an exaggerated accent.

"You take, I call, no worry, I call now."

I don't know if it was Russian, Middle Eastern, or Indian, but it was awful, and it was working. I pulled out my cell phone and dialed "DaVinci." Mike picked up the phone.

"Sir, I make pizza. It's here, in you now… yes, here in your house, I'm inside your house."

I spoke as obnoxious and loud as I possibly could. The clerk was irritated, so I attempted to hand him the phone. He dismissed me with a wave.

"Follow me."

He escorted me to the elevator, swiped his key fob, and pressed the button for DaVinci's floor.

I got to the door of the condo, rang the bell, knocked, and waited. I stood and listened. Silence. It was now or never. After a moment, I stepped back, and damn near kicked that motherfucker off the hinges.

The deadbolt ripped through the door frame. I stepped inside and shut the mangled door behind me. I chucked the pizza box on the floor, pulled a pair of black gloves out of my back pocket, and slipped them on.

The clock was ticking. I started with all the places I would hide shit if I lived here. First, I flipped over the mattress and felt around it to see if something was inside, but I came up with nothing. I checked the couch the same way. Again, nothing. There was nothing in the oven, freezer, or closet. I tore apart the entire condo before I made my way into the bathroom. I looked inside the toilet tank and then inside the exhaust vent. Nothing.

I went back into the living room to check the vents throughout the condo. I ripped them off in sections, making sure not to miss any. I kicked in the intake vent in the dining room near the floor. *Bingo.*

A small leather Louis Vuitton bag sat on the bottom right side of the vent. Inside the bag were three phones, a glass jar of exotic weed, small gold bars, cash, and a platinum chain. It was the same one he bought me when we first started working together.

The air conditioner was off, and it was hot inside DaVinci's condo. I poured sweat. Breaking, entering, and ransacking was hard work. I found what I came for. It was time to flee this crime scene. I called Mike.

"Meet me out back of the painter's house." I hung up.

Mike knew this was code for *meet me behind DaVinci's condo.*

I made my way back to the front door, but before leaving, I paused to make sure that I didn't forget anything. The pizza box was still sitting on the floor.

I have to wipe my fingerprints off that box.

I grabbed two small towels from the kitchen and wiped down the box. I stopped and looked at my work, satisfied. I couldn't help myself, though. I opened the box and stuffed a slice of pizza in my mouth. Who the fuck am I kidding? I ate two.

***

It was only a matter of time until someone came looking for the million dollars. I thought about my life and the risks I'd taken up to this point. I needed more money to reach my goal of getting my brother home from the hospital. While I had inherited a life-changing amount of money, a million dollars isn't a million dollars when it comes with a price tag.

DaVinci knew my legal name, social security number, and the names of my family members. If I had nothing to lose, you're damn right I would have taken the money and run, but I did have something to lose. Many lives, including mine, depended on what happened with that million dollars.

DaVinci may have been missing, but my loyalty, and the lessons he taught me, were still present.

I have to make this right. I have to make this right for DaVinci.

The cell phone store was my next stop. I brought the phones I had confiscated from DaVinci's condo and matched them with brand-new chargers.

When I arrived home, I plugged them in, turned them on, and waited. If I were ever going to find out what happened to DaVinci and get this money into the hands of the appropriate party, these cell phones would be the key.

A few days passed before one of the cell phones finally rang. My adrenaline kicked into high gear. Heart racing, I answered the phone.

"Hello," said a voice on the other end of the line.

"I work for DaVinci," I said.

Silence... long, awkward silence. Then, the ghost on the other end of the line replied in a distinctly Chinese accent.

"Where is DaVinci?"

"I have no idea," I said.

"You were in Vegas. You have the money. Bring it to me, or I come for it."

I tried to make a request, but he cut me off before I could speak.

"In three days, you will meet me at DeLagé Nightclub in Dallas. Come alone."

The meeting with DaVinci's connection had only three possible outcomes: death, prison, or redemption. I had no intention of going to prison, and I wasn't dead yet.

Three days later, my plane touched down at Dallas Fort Worth International Airport. I grabbed a cab and headed to a hotel to meet Mike before I went to the designated nightclub to meet DaVinci's partner. I had already taken the necessary steps to ensure the money would get to Dallas the day before my arrival. Mike was the only person I could trust to transport the money.

When I arrived in Dallas, I found Mike waiting in a hotel room for me with a snub nose .38 Special on the table. He had been guarding the money all night. If I lost that money, I would be dead.

Mike drove the rental car while I rode shotgun. We pulled into an isolated nightclub with a parking lot that wrapped around the entire building. I had him reverse the car into a spot in a far corner of the lot with a good view of the entrance.

"Stay in the car, leave the money in the trunk. I'll meet them and come back for the money when I know it's safe," I said.

"Who are you meeting?" Mike asked.

"A ghost... a ghost with a Chinese accent."

I stood in front of the club and waited. People in cowboy hats and alligator boots came and went from the club. Their passing eyes told me I didn't belong there. This was not my territory. Four Asian men in suits came outside and stood next to me. Unsure if this was them or not, I decided to say something.

"Is there something you gentleman need help with?"

"Let's go inside and talk."

We went inside and sat down. The most diminutive guy out of the four sat across from me and folded his hands on the table. I could see tattoos peeking out from the edge of his shirt cuffs. Two more guys appeared and stood behind me. I was surrounded. A terrible feeling crept over me.

I have to find DaVinci.

"Where is DaVinci?" I asked.

"You should know. You're the one who answered his phone."

"I haven't seen him since Las Vegas. He disappeared from the hotel."

The small guy across me motioned to the waitress for drinks.

"Have a beer, get a lap dance, or get laid if you want. Relax, I'll be back."

I drank my beer while I watched women dance on the stage. The music was so loud I could barely think. They wanted the money, but we had yet to discuss terms for the exchange. More importantly, I had come to return the money for DaVinci but was determined to get something out of the deal as well. I didn't like how this was going. It was taking too long. Something was off. When I slid my chair back to leave, a hand tapped me on my left shoulder.

"Let's go," one of the guys said.

"Go where?" I replied.

"The meeting's in the parking lot."

If I went outside, I'd be a dead man. I stood up.

"Tell him to come inside," I said, "I'm not going out to some parking lot. I came for a meeting that was supposed to be here."

"That's not how it works. You have no choice."

At that moment, I realized that I wasn't leaving with the money.

We went around the side of the building to an empty parking lot, where a giant pickup truck stood alone with a large man at the rear door. He was holding the bag of cash in his hand. Mike lay just behind the man with the bag, motionless, a pool of blood under his head.

"You were told to come alone," said the diminutive man.

The guys escorted me to the truck, spun me around, patted me down, and hit me hard as a brick. This wasn't my first beating, but after how long it went on, I was worried it might be my last.

I fell onto my hands and knees. Blood dripped from my head onto the pavement in front of me. Somewhere beyond the blood, probably three inches from my head, I heard a blast. Mortality laced with pistol smoke. They had my full attention now. I was abandoned by my best friend and, more importantly, by my own rationale. I forgave him and accepted my fate. Pain and suffering had become a way of life. I scarcely made out a cluster of words through the deafening silence of gunfire.

"Where the fuck's DaVinci? He owes me three million dollars," said the voice within the dust.

"I brought you the money from Las Vegas!" I yelled.

I looked over at Mike, still lying in a pool of blood. Groans of anguish escaped from his mouth.

"You're two million dollars short."

They gave me no opportunity to respond.

I have to find DaVinci.

"Kill him. Do it quick—"

"—Wait! I have DaVinci's clientele in Philadelphia. I'll get the money."

There was a long silence. The dust began to clear. Relieved, I tried to stand but was held in place.

"You have one shot."

Bullets dumped out and scattered across the pavement. One round slid back into the chamber. My future spun in the cylinder, then snapped back into the frame.

"One shot will determine your fate."

A finite choice loaded in the pistol was laid on my left shoulder.

Mike awoke from the haze of his own dark fate and reached toward me, "Don't—

His voice was light years away.

I thought of everything I loved in this world.

I took the gun and put it to my head.

I thought of Vinny, I thought of Sammy, and I thought of Lana. At that moment, an unexpected and terrifying thought burned through my consciousness.

Who am I?

I pulled the trigger.

There was no white light. No sense of peace. Nothing final, just the luck of an empty chamber.

A pair of hands picked me up, put me on my feet, and placed a phone in my hand.

"You earned your shot. Leave before I change my mind."

As I walked back from the brink of death, a voice called out to me with sobering clarity. "Your name is pain, and life is suffering."

Had I spoken out loud?

I looked up and saw the trace of a woman. Her luminescent skin shimmered under a street light across the parking lot. She possessed a glittering, surreal quality. She was dressed in clothing so antiquated that it could only have been rendered in a century before my time.

Holding Mike around my shoulder, I wiped the blood from my eyes to get a better look. As I hobbled past her, she appeared to flicker in and out of reality. A one-dimensional figure in the three-dimensional world. Motionless, she met eyes with me. A mysterious smile emerged.

***

The last time I disappeared on Lana was when I went to jail after the car chase with DaVinci in Northeast Philadelphia. Lana wasn't my one phone call. Instead, I called Mike to look for DaVinci. I spent three long days in the 15th District jail while she spent three days worried sick. After the asbestos incident, I promised her she would be my one phone call if I ever got arrested or into trouble. I had broken that promise and, in turn, shattered her trust.

Lana wasn't the cliche of a girlfriend who sat at home complaining that her boyfriend wasn't around enough. Those women only exist in books and movies. In real life, every woman has their own heart, their own mind, and their own story. And her story was just as important as mine. She had her own problems, her own sick relatives, her own broken family, and painful memories. My story was no different, and it certainly wasn't a reason to justify my neglect of her. Lana lived her life with purpose. She had a positive impact on the world. My life was out of control. I brought nothing but chaos. Lana worked in the emergency room every night, saving lives. She may have even been working to save people's lives in car accidents that I may have caused during one of the many high-speed chases.

I spent a week in a hotel in Texas, recovering from my beating. I lacked the courage to call and tell her what had happened. Her calls came pouring into my cell phone, but I never answered.

On my way home from Texas, I thought about how Lana would react when she saw my face. I knew in my heart, it was over. I prayed she would forgive me.

"I can't do this anymore."

She spoke to me quietly and averted her eyes as I came through the front door. I knew she couldn't bear to see the damage to my face. I couldn't bear to look at myself. I hung my head.

"You promised me you would get out. It's been years."

"I'm in too deep now. I can't walk away."

It was true. I was in too deep, but what I said didn't matter. Nothing was going to change her mind.

She packed her bags and moved out of the house that night. Lana stopped in the doorway.

"Money isn't everything. Love has no price tag."

My ego got the best of me. I found myself raising my voice at her.

"A man who can't be bought is priceless!"

I wanted to be right. While there was some truth to what I said it had no relevance in that conversation. I didn't care and my impulse demanded that I get the last word in. The truth though, is that I was wrong. That momentary, fleeting satisfaction of feeling right, like Lana, was gone.

I had fought the whole world my entire life to find love and I traded it in for a week of misery in a run-down motel room outside of Dallas, Texas.

21.

I left the motel surrounded by a motorcade of Asians. On the drive back to Philly, I called in every favor I could to get the product sold as fast as possible. I sold twice the amount I told them I could at the cost of not making a profit, but for me, it was about establishing a business connection. And, of course, not getting murdered.

Apparently, on the day DaVinci disappeared in Las Vegas, he was supposed to acquire money from an additional party before the meeting.

His supplier was expecting an additional two million dollars, which had vanished along with DaVinci. I had walked into the meeting in Dallas with only a third of the capital I needed to pay the debt. I have no idea why DaVinci didn't tell me that he was supposed to pick up an additional two million dollars. I paid DaVinci's debt in twenty-one days.

Within a few months, my business arrangement with Texas became so successful that I began to incorporate other parties and expand across borders. I moved into multiple condos in different cities nationwide, all secure buildings with doormen and full amenities. The more money I made, the more paranoid and isolated I became.

I thought of Lana almost every day, even though she was long gone from my life. Shortly after she left me, she moved to New York and changed her number. Although I kept tabs on her, we hadn't spoken since the day she packed her bags and moved out.

I had achieved everything I'd ever wanted and made more money than I had ever thought possible. I was on the cusp of being as successful as DaVinci. Instead of getting out of the business, I reinvested and pushed further into a life of crime, because enough was never enough.

The more that I desire and the more that I acquire, the more pain that I inherit.

When I was younger and broke the law, it was fun, but now that it had become a full-time job, it had lost its appeal. My success never felt like true success without DaVinci. I never stopped looking for him. I kept my ear to the street but got no leads. He may as well have been a figment of my imagination.

I didn't like meeting women at bars. I missed coming home to Lana. I didn't like traveling across the country alone. I preferred traveling with DaVinci. My life had become barren of family and friends. I lived in a world of unknowns, and my closest connections were shady business partners in foreign lands. I spent most of my time outside of Philadelphia. I barely even got to see Mike anymore. He decided it was best to keep his distance from me after the incident behind the club outside of Dallas. The only person who didn't have the option to cut me out of their life was Sammy, who was confined to a hospital bed.

***

I had almost acquired enough money to purchase a million-dollar home and pay for twenty-four-hour at-home care for Sammy for the rest of his life. I went to visit him during the peak of my success to share the good news with him.

"I'm close to getting you out of here, Sammy. I have it all planned out. I'm going to move you into a huge new house with twenty-four-hour care. Private nurse. No more strangers, no more hospitals."

"How are you going to pay for all of this?"

"I have one more deal to do, and then I'm done. It'll be enough to set us up for life."

The nurse came in to administer his daily medication. We waited until she left to continue our conversation.

"Why can't you stop now?" Sammy asked.

I was twenty-two years old and had already lived the lives of a thousand men. Yet my life had only amounted to a handful of meaningless minutes. I was lost in crime, and I had outrun myself.

"I'm running out of time," I said. "My friends are all dead, locked up, or hooked on drugs."

"It's not your fault," he said.

"It is my fault, Sammy. It's all my fault. I should have stopped you from getting into the car that night."

"It was my choice. I fucked my life up. Not you."

"Either way, I'm going to fix it for you. I'm going to fix it for us."

I held back tears. I knew in my heart that something wasn't right, but the wheels were already in motion. I wanted to stop, but I couldn't.

"I have to do it, Sammy. I have to."

I needed to hear it from him. I wanted him to justify my actions... so I asked him.

"What would you do if I were in that bed instead of you?"

He paused. Thoughts of an older brother's guidance weighed in his mind.

"I'd do the same fucking thing."

***

This job was going to be big, three-point-five million big. I needed to assemble a team to carry the workload across the border in the middle of the country, drop the work in Chicago, and then bring the cash home.

I headed north across the border and met with the team at a warehouse in a rural location. The team consisted of three other guys and me. I had hired them through a third party in Philadelphia.

We spent the day sealing and sanitizing the product to ensure no scent or residue was left outside the load. We planned to rendezvous at the warehouse the following day at midnight and pick up our packs. To reduce our losses if one of us got caught, we would split up and use GPS-guided routes to cross the border at different entry points. We closed the shop for the night and returned to our respective hotels.

Before returning to my hotel, I stopped at a local restaurant and ordered a steak and a beer.

"I'm sorry, I need to see some ID for the beer," the waitress said.

I had no ID because there could be no record of my having been there, and this was certainly something that I couldn't explain to her.

"I don't have it. Never mind."

"Are you sure? Do you live nearby, want to run and grab it?"

"By nearby, do you mean twelve hundred miles away?"

She laughed, and I pushed the issue no further. My meal came, and as I ate my food, I looked around the room and realized I was the only one dining by myself. I listened to the chatter from nearby tables. The clink of a glass and silverware. The sounds of a healthy social life. To this day, I still wish that I had that beer.

The warehouse stood alone in an empty field, illuminated only by a single floodlight. Besides our contact, I was the first to arrive. My pack was on a table next to the others along the wall. It was positioned the same way I had left it the night before. I inspected it to ensure that no one had handled it. Nothing had changed.

The team gathered to go over the final details. Four guys, four packs, four routes, and four lives that would instantly transform if they made it across the border.

We suited up, and everything was in order, but DaVinci's seven rules for success told me otherwise.

DaVinci's fourth rule: *Separate the money from the drugs.*

The team had demanded to be paid upfront. I brought their payment to the warehouse where the product was stored. This was the first time I directly violated any one of DaVinci's rules.

DaVinci's fifth rule: *Never say you have it unless you have it in hand.*

I operated under constant misdirection. Yet, I called the Chicago contact to inform him that the shipment would arrive the following day. This was a major violation because communicating your arrival time allowed the possibility of someone tipping off the authorities about your movements. Still, it was the only way the Chicago connection would allow the deal to go down.

DaVinci's seventh rule: *Limit your exposure.*

My fixation on the size of the score and obsession with money put me in a compromised and vulnerable position. I should not have been in that warehouse. On every similar transaction before this one, I had directed the deal from a cell phone hundreds of miles away. I made less money on those deals, but I operated from a much safer place.

DaVinci's sixth rule: *Never rush.*

I didn't vet these guys. I had hired them from a third-party source, a guy named Philthy Phil. I was told they were reliable, but I wasn't given any information about their backgrounds or identities. Normally, I had a contact in the judicial system who would run the names of the people I was planning to work with. This kept me up to date on who had been arrested and who might be cooperating with the authorities.

I didn't know anything about these guys. I looked across the warehouse and saw the crew standing in a huddle. A terrible calm swept through my body. I walked up to them.

"Lift your shirts," I said.

Everybody froze. You could hear a pin drop. The first two guys lifted their shirts without a problem, but the third guy refused.

"I'm not lifting my shirt."

The other two guys looked at him, then back at me. He felt pressured, and reluctantly, he lifted his shirt.

This dumb fuck.

DaVinci's third rule: *No guns.*

"Get rid of it," I said.

"No fucking way. I don't know you."

"My point exactly. I'm not asking."

"What do you want me to do with it?" he asked.

"I don't care. Just get rid of it."

He disappeared outside and returned twenty minutes later without the gun. I grabbed my pack and said, "Let's go."

Nothing could stop me now. Fear had vanished years ago on that rainy night in Philadelphia.

***

We stepped into the cold of the night. I stared into the void of a snow-covered landscape. We lined up as if preparing for battle. Once we started, it would be a mad dash over the border. We made one final check of our satellite phones and GPS routes.

I broke into a steady jog, maintaining my steps and pacing. The weight of the pack pulled down on my shoulders with every stride. The snow was deep. I fought through the terrain and came to a clearing. This was the part of my route in which I would be most exposed. At the edge of the clearing, I felt a vibration in my pocket. That satellite phone was only supposed to ring if we ran into trouble. It was Philthy Phil.

"I had no choice. I'm sorry. You were always a good dude to me, but I was facing three strikes. I'm sorry, I'm sorry, man," he said. The line went dead.

Philthy Phil... you fucking dirtbag.

I can't say that I was surprised. In a way, I had been waiting for that phone call my entire life. I had violated every one of DaVinci's rules. It was only a matter of time before it all came crashing down. I guess now was as good a time as any. My odds of escaping this were slim to none, but I would try anyway. Deep in the night, I saw the lights of the border patrol fanning out across the forest. I could hear the sound of barking dogs in the distance. Time was running out. They were closing in.

I dropped my pack on the ground in the middle of the moonlit clearing and opened it. I pulled out a bottle of lighter fluid and a road flare. I drenched the backpack and placed the empty bottle on top. This was my moment of truth. I popped the cap at the end of the flare and dropped it on the backpack. Flames exploded into the sky. I felt the heat on my face, a fortune on fire.

Time slowed, and I stood like a child in the warmth of a campfire, watching it burn. My heart swelled with contentment. A sense of peace flowed through me.

What, if anything, do I desire?

Amidst the crackle of the flames, a voice came to me and spoke clearly.

"So that's it, huh? This is how it ends?"

I peered past the pillar of flames into the darkness of the trees at the edge of the clearing. I saw a world of smoke beyond the focus plane. I was looking into a landscape without lines or borders.

***

Fire and pain scorched through my muscles as I sprinted away from the flames and into the trees. With every stride, adrenaline, determination, and resolve mixed in my veins. I reached deep down inside for something extra. I felt an incredible rush of euphoria. If you've never felt this type of euphoria before, then you've never been pushed to the edge.

The faster I ran, the more the sweat poured down. I suffocated inside my layers of clothing. The icy air burned my lungs through my ski mask. Plumes of smoke expelled from my mouth. I sprinted towards two trees that stood side by side like pillars. As I ran between them, they transformed into a passage between two parked cars.

I was back in the blistering heat of the Philadelphia summer, bolting through an alleyway, trying to buy enough time for DaVinci to escape. Kids shooting water guns ran through backyards as classic rock played in the distance.

In the icy cold of the Canadian winter, my past was catching up to my present. I could feel the agents getting closer, but I wouldn't surrender easily. The other side of the clearing brought me to a broad and shallow stream. Hoping to throw the dogs off my scent, I plunged into the freezing water. Euphoric overload.

I ducked between cars, trying not to get hit by traffic as it whizzed by me on Cottman Avenue. I slipped and caught myself with my hand on the pavement. I could feel the sting of the road rash. Police sirens screamed behind me.

I opened my eyes and looked at the clear night sky above me. There wasn't a star in sight. I lay on my back on a bed of rocks and snow, blood pouring from a cut on my hand. My clothes were soaked, doubling their weight. I couldn't run anymore. I had been running my whole life.

Eight customs officers drew their weapons and surrounded me. I recognized one of them. It was the guy from the warehouse with the gun. Dogs and officers both barked commands at me.

"Get the fuck on the ground!"

I didn't have an ounce of energy left in my body. I couldn't move if I wanted to.

"I'm already on the ground. I can't get any further onto the ground," I muttered.

FALL

22.

DaVinci's first rule: *Don't get arrested.*

DaVinci's second rule: *Don't get arrested.*

I thought that burning the evidence would help my legal case... 18 U.S.C. § 371 said otherwise.

18 U.S.C. § 371 states that "[i]f two or more persons conspire either to commit any offense against the United States or to defraud the United States or any agency thereof in any manner or for any purpose," you will be seeing, feeling, and experiencing the full punishment of the law.

In other words, if you see the word "conspiracy" on a piece of paper with your name on it, you're fucked.

I was angry at myself because I knew better, yet here I was, handcuffed and under arrest. This was the end of my life as I knew it and the beginning of a judiciary game that would never end. The Federal guidelines for punishment aren't dictated by the crime committed alone. They also consider how many offenses you have been convicted of as well as your criminal history.

Conspiracy is an ambiguous law that ensures a conviction for anyone unlucky enough to be caught in its web. As a young man, I was in the last place I wanted to be. It was a complex matrix of legalities, perspectives, and versions of the truth.

From the moment you are arrested, your life is about survival, pure survival. I was thousands of miles away from home, and passing through this machine unscathed would be a test of my perseverance.

The intake process into a maximum-security prison is exhausting. Paperwork, paperwork, paperwork. Including a waiver that I had to sign, which said I couldn't sue the prison if my life came to an untimely end during my incarceration.

Orange jumpers and Bruce Lee slippers were my new dress code. Nothing makes you feel more vulnerable than wearing adult pajamas and a cheap pair of sneakers with no laces.

I walked onto the cell block with a bedroll across my arms. I could see the other inmates sizing me up. I saw blank faces driven by anger and impulse. I decided it was best to keep to myself.

Bob Barker's toothbrush, Bob Barker's hygiene, Bob Barker's everything. I washed my face, looked at my four-inch toothbrush and one-inch deodorant made by Bob Barker, and said to myself, Bob Barker, you've got one sick sense of humor. This, of course, wasn't the same Bob Barker from *The Price Is Right*. Some other Bob Barker thought it would be a good idea to plaster his name all over the hygiene products that he supplied for prisoners.

As I lay awake that night, I panned how I would abscond from justice. Go to court, make bail, and run. A single thought played over and over in my mind.

I have to get out of here.

We were taken downstairs at six a.m. to an eating area. The breakfast trays were brought out as we sat down at cold stainless steel tables. An inmate who worked as a porter served us breakfast. When a tray was placed in front of me, I wanted to throw it at the wall. Oatmeal water, or what looked like white puke and snot combined, was for breakfast. I slid it back across the table and said, "Thanks, but no thanks."

A correctional officer's voice came over the loudspeaker.

Court, inmates for court. Get ready for court.

We were escorted back down to the intake area, searched, shackled, and loaded into a tiny van headed for court. Cramped between inmates with bad breath and body odor, the ride to the courthouse was claustrophobic. Through the caged windows of the van, I caught a glimpse of a sign that read *United States Courthouse* as we pulled into a secure underground parking garage. We were stopped at a security booth by armed guards as we entered. Garage doors dropped down behind the van, locking us in. The van doors opened, and the marshals yelled out like drill sergeants as they assigned us our Bureau Of Prisons inmate numbers. Eight numbers replaced my name.

"Do not! Forget! Your number! It is how we find you! Memorize it, write it down, take it on a date, tattoo it, have a kid with it because you're fucking married to it... Forever!"

I met my lawyer about five minutes before entering the courtroom.

"You're going to have to make bail," she said. "The other guys you were arrested with are being released."

I was shuffled into the courtroom with no preparation or information I could use to help convince the judge to give me bail. An elderly female stenographer with a beehive hairdo sat on my left as I walked in. Another beehive hairdo. The disciplinary world seemed to be populated by women with beehive hairdos and men with perfect hair parts. A Texas longhorn skull mounted on the wall peered down at me.

Other inmates and I sat in the jurors' chairs while we waited for our arraignments. I did my best not to trip on my shackles as I made my way to the podium. I was asked to please state my name and inmate number. I did, and then the charges were read aloud. I was being indicted for conspiracy to commit drug trafficking. That's not the part I heard, however. What caught my ear was the part about ten to forty years and a five million dollar fine. Ten to forty years? Five million dollars? I wasn't even aware that such lengthy sentences or fines existed for conspiracy to commit drug trafficking.

This can't be happening.

I had an active bench warrant in Philadelphia for the high-speed car chase with DaVinci. Evidently, when my fingerprints were taken for this case, it flagged the Philadelphia police department and helped them solve the mystery of Nick Whottin's true identity. My bail was denied. I was granted a follow-up hearing in which my opportunity for bail would be reconsidered if I could remove my open warrant in Philadelphia.

***

Every phone call in prison is monitored and dissected by Federal agents. This made getting a message out extremely difficult. The only person who would be able to understand what I was saying was my friend Mike. He was as well-versed in street terminology and misdirection as I was.

A pre-recorded message from a robotic voice came on over the phone.

This is a pre-paid call from an inmate at a Federal prison. Press one to accept.

"Hello," Mike answered.

"What's up, Mike?"

"Dude, where the fuck are you calling me from?"

"Doesn't matter. I need you to listen. Can you do that?"

"Of course, whatever you need."

I spoke to Mike in code.

"Do you remember the two sisters, Mona and Lisa Di Ser Piero, that lived in that high-rise downtown?" I asked.

Translation: *Do you remember where DaVinci lives?*

"I remember them. A wild bunch of ladies," Mike replied.

Translation: *Yes, that guy who was involved in some dangerous shit.*

"I need you to try and find Mona for me, please. I stopped by to see her when she was pregnant, but she wasn't home. So, I grabbed pizza around the corner. The baby's foot in the womb was knocking on it. Do you remember the day I called you?"

Translation: *Do you remember when I called you and told you not to answer the phone when I kicked in DaVinci's door after he went missing?*

"Yes, once upon a time in Mexico with a bike chain."

Translation: *Yes, when you kicked in DaVinci's door and paid me with a Platinum chain to pick you up downtown.*

"Start with her and see if you can find out where Lisa lives. I never got her new address or her sister's phone number. Always getting drunk at that bar, Birdland, and singing *Message In A Bottle* at the top of their lungs."

Translation: *Find out where DaVinci is because I never did. If not, call his connections in that black book I left with you. I need urgent help. It's bad.*

"I'll stop by the bar, maybe get some pizza, and see if anyone knows anything. Don't worry. I'm on it."

Translation: *I'll go through the book and go downtown to his condo.*

"Thanks, man. Love you. I'll find the combo to a metal box," I said.

Translation: *I'll call you when it's safe.*

"Are you gonna be okay?" Mike asked.

Translation: *Are you going to be in prison for a long time?*

"I'm not sure, but right now, I'm fucked."

Translation: *I'm not sure, but right now, I'm fucked.*

***

Over the next few months, most of my time was spent on the phone with my lawyers in Philly. What can be done in five minutes at home takes you a whole day in prison. Anything simple becomes impossible. The open warrant in Philly was the only thing standing between me and a bail release for my current Federal charges.

Regarding the Feds and pretrial release, it's as serious as it gets. The options for me were either a cash payment or a third-party collateral bond. These often include stipulations of house arrest and intense monitoring from pretrial services. If you even look like a flight risk or there's a chance you're going to run, it's a guaranteed denial of bail.

Miraculously, I was able to reach the District Attorney in Philly. My request to him was simple. Please drop the warrant. I said nothing about being guilty. I told him I wouldn't fight the case to encourage him to lift this simple yet monumental bench warrant. I said I needed to get my affairs in order because it looked like I was going to prison for a long time. The District Attorney was willing to lift my warrant because I had no prior convictions. I thanked him, hung up, and called my lawyer to push for my release. My lawyer filed the appropriate motions, and after six months, I was set to appear in front of the judge for a new bail hearing.

The night before my hearing, I lay awake thinking about my life and the actions that led me to be locked inside a nine-by-eleven prison cell. Lana left me, DaVinci disappeared on me, and I failed to keep my promise to Sammy. The only persistent thought beyond my kaleidoscope of personal failures was to get out of prison, grab a fake passport, and abscond to Europe to avoid prosecution.

I walked into the courtroom again past the clerk with the beehive hairdo and the Texas longhorn skull. The judge entered and asked the prosecution to run my name through the NCIC (National Crime Information

Center). Sure as hell, the damn warrant in Philly was still active. The District Attorney failed to keep his word. The judge denied my bail and any other option for my release. It was solidified forever. Running to Europe was no longer an option. My plan to flee was nothing more than a mirage.

My lawyer came to visit me a few months after the hearing. Only then did I begin to grasp the true gravity of my situation. I'd never heard of a mandatory minimum sentence, nor did I have any knowledge of how the Federal sentencing guidelines worked. It was a lot for me to learn, and at twenty-two years old, I was overwhelmed. She explained that if I decided to exercise my constitutional rights and go to trial and lose, I would likely receive a longer sentence than if I had taken a plea deal. When the average defendant goes to trial and loses, they are sentenced to approximately three times the length of the punishment they would've received had they pleaded guilty. She cited multiple cases where the judge had asserted that a lengthier sentence was warranted because the defendant went to trial and had wasted taxpayer dollars.

Forty years on the bad side, ten years on the good side, and eighteen years or more in the middle if I lost at trial. At my age, it was impossible to comprehend the amount of time I was facing. A year was a long time. A decade was forever. I thought about how much things had changed from the seventies to the eighties, to the nineties. Fuck me, that's a lot of time.

The Feds have roughly a ninety-five percent conviction rate leveraged in their favor with harsh mandatory minimums and sentencing guidelines set in place. A trial was a gamble that I couldn't afford to take unless I were willing to bet my life on it. The house always wins. It may not be in the law books, but rest assured, it's an unspoken rule you become acutely aware of.

Most prisoners are first-time, nonviolent drug offenders, and fortunately, I landed in this category. Still, I was going to be sentenced to ten to forty years in prison for conspiracy.

I fucked up. I fucked up bad.

From what my lawyer presented as my best-case scenario, a Hail Mary pass, and a long shot, I would serve six and a half years with good time credit and a drug treatment program to help reduce my time. As we reviewed the discovery and discussed this, I tried to compartmentalize the years in my mind. This was my desperate attempt to find a way of accepting my sentence.

I broke my possible sentence into three segments. Two years, two years, and two and a half years. That's how I would do my time rather than daily, weekly, or monthly. She also explained while I may be pleading guilty, there was no guarantee. I needed to accept that instead of the ten, I could get the forty. I asked her why I was facing such a stiff penalty. What she said next confirmed some of the things I had suspected about the system since I was a teenager.

"There is no right, there is no wrong, there is no crime, there is no punishment, it's just business."

I spent a year researching case law to try and find a legal loophole in hopes of regaining my freedom. Whenever I brought up a fact that I thought might help my case, my lawyer's response was always the same.

"Forget it."

The Federal system is almost impossible to beat unless you know how it operates from the inside out, which would only help you move around it a bit better at best. The more I learned about the system, the more I thought about the worst-case scenario. I could do nothing except choose one of three options: escape, serve my time, or kill myself.

***

Living in the unknown was as stressful as knowing that I was going to prison, if not worse. Time slowed down, stood still, and eventually dissolved.

The night before my sentencing, I went to my cell and read the notes I had jotted down in preparation for my court appearance. Through a four-inch window next to my bed, I watched the sunset in its entirety.

I thought of my mom that night and the life she had endured with her children. One son was dead, one son was permanently disabled, and one son was on drugs. The only thing missing was one son in prison, I guess, that one son was me.

God had always watched over me. If he hadn't, I would have been dead a long time ago. It was time to make peace with the man upstairs. I knelt, bowed my head, and prayed.

"Give me a break. I'll fly straight and get a job. No more crime, no more hustling, I'll even go to temple. No, not the college in North Philly, but the real one this time. Can we do seven? I'll be happy with seven, six, maybe six, God?"

I opened one eye. No divine intervention or miracle had occurred, so I prayed harder.

"Listen, God, let's sit down, have a few cold beers, and talk this out like men. Maybe talk to Jesus. I met him briefly in grade school. He knows I'm not a bad guy. Six... can we do six? I'll be happy with six."

I opened both eyes and looked around the cell. Nothing. I prayed even harder.

"You know what. I got greedy. I apologize. I'm under a lot of stress, as you can imagine. Let's stick with the seven. I'm good with the seven. Is this thing on? Testing, testing. Are you there, Lord?"

As the evening continued, I sat on a hard plastic chair at a concrete desk, praying into the late hours of the night. I sincerely asked God for forgiveness, but the bitter truth was that my negotiations with him were simply a way for me to psychologically manage the loss of my youth.

The next morning, I sat on a wooden bench in a holding cell at the end of a short hallway. The courtroom entrance was nearly out of earshot, but I could still hear the carnage from within. Men wore brave faces but quickly turned grey when their names were called. I watched them enter the courtroom as men and come back out through that same doorway as shadows of their former selves, drained of all life and emotion. I was next.

I heard only the sound of my heartbeat as I walked toward the defendant's chair. One by one, they read the list of charges aloud from my open case in Philly. The prosecution asked for an upward departure. They felt ten years wasn't enough time for me, and adding another five years would be a more appropriate place to start. Open case or not, I was never convicted of any crime as an adult, and the judge asked that very question to the prosecutor.

"Has he been convicted of any of these charges?"

"No, Your Honor."

"Then why are you bringing this up to me? There will be no upward departure granted here today."

When the proceedings reached the point where it was time for me to address the court, I handed my lawyer back the speech we had prepared together. She shook her head in disapproval.

"Your Honor, men have stood in the same spot, in the same cuffs, in the same situation, pleading for their lives. Desperate to legitimize their actions, not for the pursuit of change, but for a sentence reduction. I'm not brave. I'm remorseful. My lawyer advised me not to speak freely. Please forgive me in advance. I have one chance and I'm at my best when I speak from my heart. I look around today... no brothers, no family, and no friends. Not one person showed up or wrote a letter on my behalf to say that I'm not a bad guy."

My eyes teared up. I composed myself and refused to cry.

"I'd like to tell you that I came from the bottom. I came from the worst. I came from the abused, beaten, left for dead, and forgotten. That would be motive enough, but the truth is, I fucked up, I broke the law because I was good at it. So, it's just me today, Your Honor, standing here, doing my best to tell you that I'm not a bad guy, but I look around with no one to confirm that, and I simply don't believe it anymore. I am a bad guy, and I deserve what's coming."

One hundred and ten months came crashing down over my skull. Years of my life were erased in a matter of seconds. Both feet left the ground as truth flooded the deepest parts of my mind. Dark reality bled into the corners of my eyes. I no longer had possession of my life.

I expected relief after hearing my prison sentence, but my lawyer never explained that I would be sentenced in months and not years. I found myself in a state of panic. Losing consciousness, my lawyer noticed my weakened demeanor and hurried to translate. She scribbled a note on a piece of paper and slid it over for me to read.

Nine years and two months. No parole.

Nine years and two months ago, I was fourteen years old— barely a teenager. I was still running around my neighborhood on a bike, buying dollar slices of pizza, chasing girls, and collecting baseball cards. Nine years and two months was three times the length of my adult life thus far.

Obliged to show gratitude to the courts for the nine years and two months I had received, I politely uttered, "Thank you, Your Honor."

"Take him away," she replied.

A million thoughts raced through my head. Is there a light in this darkness? What possible good can come from my incarceration? I would enter prison as myself, but would that memory, that version of me, survive long enough to live again?

The drive back to the holding facility from the court was through a few city blocks during the daytime hustle and bustle, but for me, life had gone quiet. That wasn't me. That didn't happen. Someone else just got sentenced to that awful amount of time. To be shocked about something that I knew would happen was an odd feeling. In my heart, I could never accept it.

I re-entered my cell block. The inmates were loud. Two of them fought, I hardly noticed as I made my way through the concrete jungle to the pay phones.

Through the thick and into the clear, I reached for the phone. In an attempt to stitch my heart back together, my first call was a short one to my brother Sammy. It rang and rang. His reduction of motor skills as a result of the accident made a simple task such as picking up a phone extremely difficult. I ended up calling a few times in a row before he could manage to answer correctly.

This is a pre-paid call from an inmate at a Federal prison. Press one to accept.

"He... hel... hello," Sammy mumbled.

I smiled when I heard his voice. "Sammy, how are you?"

"I'm okay. Where are you calling from? Are you coming to visit me today?"

Sammy's head trauma had left him with continuous memory loss problems. My body went cold. I began to shake. With his medical condition, I knew there was a chance I'd never get to see him again before I got out of prison.

"I just got back from court," I said.

"What happened?"

"I tried. I really did, but I failed you. I got one hundred and ten months."

"For what?"

"Conspiracy to commit drug trafficking."

"How long is that?"

"Just over nine years."

"I'm sorry, little bro. That's a lot of time."

"I fucked up. I thought I could get you out of there. I believed I could fix it all."

"I never needed you to do all that for me. I only needed your phone calls and visits."

When he said these words, I realized how little appreciation I had for my life in the free world. I was never missing anything. I had only tried to convince myself that I was in order to justify my actions. At that moment, I looked at my life for the first time and understood that it had value, not just to myself but also to the people who loved me.

"I feel awful, Sammy. I'll never make a mistake like this again. Never."

"Just know that there will come a day when you walk out of there. Keep calling me. I love you, little bro."

"I love you too." I hung up the phone and went to work out.

I was relieved to know it was nine years. Sick, I know, but the psychological desperation of wanting to go to prison became my way of life. It became a way of life for all of us there.

When I hit the pull-up bars that day, something was different. I felt lighter. The weight of not knowing the length of my sentence had been lifted from my shoulders. I was finally free to be a prisoner.

23.

Twenty-four hours a day, we lived in tight quarters under extreme pressure and high tension, a perfect recipe for a maximum-stress environment. We did get some recreation outside on the roof in a small cement cube with a regulated blue sky for a ceiling. Now that I had been sentenced, I began to reclaim the pieces of my personality that I had suppressed over the last eighteen months. I tried to keep a light heart and make jokes whenever possible. I had no interest in bitterness, resentment, or misery. I refused to become institutionalized.

Between the outside yard and the gym, there was a hallway that the inmates used as a makeshift barbershop. I cut hair to stay busy while I waited to be shipped off to a long-term prison, where I would serve the remainder of my time.

A guy who had just been arrested for murder sat in my chair. Lucky me.

"Give me a low fade and one inch on the top," he said.

"No problem, buddy, you got it."

He began to tell me why he was there.

I didn't ask, I don't care, and I don't want to know.

"What had happened was... I was drinking and ran out of beer, so I went to the gas station to buy more. When I was inside, someone looked in the back of my truck and saw a dead body wrapped inside of a rug. I didn't kill him. I mean, I was there, but I didn't kill him. Do you think I'm going to be okay?"

"No, dude, you're not, and I'd stop talking about your case in here."

"My lawyer told me there are witnesses that will testify that I did it."

"That sucks. Tough break, I guess."

"Do you know how to get stuff in here?" he asked.

"Possibly. What do you need, cigarettes, weed?"

"No, heroin."

"How much are you looking for?"

"Enough to kill me."

Zzzz... vroom. My clippers sounded like a warplane going in for a hard dive across the back of his head. You know in the movies how people spit water out from shock? Well, this ain't that. Instead, my abrupt move with the clippers made his hair resemble the 1988 New York Stock Exchange.

"What was that?" he asked.

"Ummm, nothing," I replied.

"Does it look all right?"

"Not really. It looks like you're guilty," I said.

"What?"

"Oh, you meant your hair? My bad, ahh... yeah... It's fine. I got it."

For the rest of my time there, I swore I heard the sound of an airplane diving every time I saw him around the prison. I nicknamed him the Kamikaze Pilot. Oddly enough, the name stuck, and he liked it.

***

I wrote letters twice a week to the Bureau Of Prisons in Grand Prairie, Texas, requesting I be moved from this holding facility and into a long-term prison. After I harassed them for a few months, I began my transit to an FCI (Federal Correctional Institution), where I would serve the remainder of my time.

The Bureau Of Prisons doesn't give you advance notice. There is no warning. One day, a CO knocks on your cell door and says, "Pack your shit."

The process of pressing you into the mold of an ideal inmate begins at four a.m. Transit is a mechanism built to do one thing. Churn out meat. One by one, we stepped out of the holding tank and signed out of custody. We spent hours waiting. I skipped eating and intentionally dehydrated myself because the bathroom was only a mirage now.

The marshals drove us to a remote prison along the southeast border of Texas. I waited there over the next few months before going back into transit.

My next stop was an I.C.E. (Immigration Customs Enforcement) facility in the middle of nowhere. Fifty of us were crammed into a ten-man cell. Super tight, I mean nuts to butts tight, and for some reason, when you're in transit, although you're dehydrated, you always have to pee. I was lucky enough to snag a seat in the holding tank, and I stayed there until my pupils turned yellow. Nobody talked as we stood still in that torturous space for five hours, marinating in gaseous fecal clouds.

After hours of waiting, I couldn't hold it, and believe me when I tell you, peeing in a phone booth is no easy task. I apologized profusely to the inmates around me. Excuse me, sir, can you get your head out of my way? You're blocking my shot.

The marshals came and retrieved us once more to go back into transit. We headed north. Fuck me. I had to pee again. I yelled out to the sheriff, "Pull over, or I'm gonna lose it all over the floor of this van!"

"You better not!" the sheriff yelled.

"I'm not Clint Eastwood in *Escape From Alcatraz*! What am I going to do, sprint across three hundred miles of desert with no water?"

The sheriff reluctantly broke the no-stop policy. Inmates who were too afraid to speak up were grateful that my refusal got them a bathroom break. I shuffled down the road in waist, ankle, and wrist shackles to find a lovely stretch of highway to mark my territory. The metal dug deep into my ankles as I ran the longest marathon of my life, moving at eight inches per hour. I stopped, dropped, and flowed.

During this moment of euphoria, my ears began to pick up on a noise I assumed could only be my shackles rattling in the wind. Oh, how wrong I was. I looked down to find myself in the presence of a behemoth rattlesnake. Terrified is an understatement. I changed speed from inches to centimeters and slowly backed up, returning to the transit van.

I climbed back into the van with a deeper appreciation for nature. I enjoyed the view of nothing for the rest of our three-hour drive through a barren wasteland. That's when I saw it.

What. The. Fuck.

We pulled back into the same small town, down the same damn street, to the same damn holding facility where I had been housed just a few months earlier. I made my way back into the intake area. I was lost in a desert of concrete and steel, this time with the sound of rattlesnakes in my ears.

***

We were driven to the back of an airfield about fifteen minutes from the holding facility. A pale white beat-to-shit and I mean fifteen years ago beat-to-shit, flying deathtrap sat run down on the tarmac.

Created in 1995 and managed by the U.S. Marshals Service, the Justice Prisoner and Alien Transportation System (JPATS) is the agency responsible for transporting convicted criminals. Since the term *con* is slang for a convict, JPATS was nicknamed *Con Air*. Con Air is so old that when you first see it, you immediately imagine horrific plane crash sequences from Hollywood movies.

My eyes scanned the plane's exterior as I stood on the tarmac. I could see duct tape around some of the windows.

Before we boarded, the marshals spread themselves around the outside of the plane and broke into an improvisational ensemble with shotguns in hand.

I climbed the stairs to the cabin and stepped onto the plane. As I made my way to my seat, I asked the flight attendant, "Excuse me, what is the in-flight movie today?"

"It's called *Sit Down And Shut The Fuck Up*."

The flight attendants were actually marshals with shotguns and parachutes mounted behind them on the cabin wall. The interior of the plane was a cesspool of mold and exhaust fumes.

As I sat down in the filth, I noticed the seats looked like lazy boy recliners with distressed silhouettes of bodies that had spent too many drunk nights passed out in them. The chair your mother hated, but your dad refused to throw away, was the age-old argument where I parked my ass for the next ninety minutes.

Of course, middle seat, fuck my life! I sat in between two gentlemen. One was in prison for credit card fraud, the other for manufacturing homemade dynamite. Mr. Dynamite came across to me like a dollar-store Kaczynski who probably carried a rusty starter pistol and plastic bullwhip. He behaved like a caricature of Indiana Jones, only played by Mickey Rourke on Chinese amphetamines. Late Mickey Rourke, of course, long after he appeared in *Rumble Fish* and *Body Heat*. I tried to distract myself and calm my nerves. The Captain's voice came across the loudspeaker.

This is ahhhhh, your Captain speaking with service today headed to Oklahoma City. Welcome back, seventy percent of you, and thank you for flying Con Air. Ahhhhh, if you hear my frustrated, self-loathing voice right now, it means you royally fucked up. We are currently about ten minutes from making sure none of you attempt to escape. Due to the multiple ahhhhh, shackles around you, we ask that you look at your seatbelt and imagine it fastened securely around your waist. No need to worry about upright seats or tray tables because if you could reach them, it would only be an impressive feat of dexterity to observe. The weather doesn't matter because, upon arrival at your destination, you'll be locked inside of a building for ahhhhh, years to co me.

I laid my head back and drifted off to sleep as the plane ascended.

Rain poured down in the summer heat. Steam rose from the hot concrete. Armed with a bulletproof vest and a 9mm handgun, I approached the house from an alleyway. I stepped onto the porch and kicked in the back door. I rushed inside, desperately searching for the missing piece of the puzzle. I had spent years of my life trying to solve this mystery, and I wasn't about to give up now. I looked around the living room. A man was hidden in the corner behind a door. For a moment, I thought it was my reflection in a mirror on the wall until I noticed he wore a ski mask.

White flashes filled the air. An explosion of gunfire erupted in my direction. Brief strobes of light exposed the gunman in full view. Bullets zipped past me. Point- blank, I opened fire in his direction. He collapsed on the floor. I approached him cautiously as he bled out on the carpet. He was face down. I rolled the body over and pulled off the mask. It was DaVinci. I had killed DaVinci.

***

The wheels hit the pavement and jolted me awake. I was still incarcerated. We landed at an airfield connected to a massive complex somewhere in rural Oklahoma. Considering the volume of inmates that moved through it every day, the Oklahoma City Federal Transfer Center was run impeccably. I completed my intake process and was on the holding block within a few hours. I made my way to the phone.

This is a pre-paid call from an inmate at a Federal prison. Press one to accept.

"Hello?"

"Hi, Mrs. Weisman. I appreciate you taking my call, considering it's coming from a prison. Do you know who this is?"

"Yes, I remember you."

"I ended up getting in trouble, which is why your daughter left me, but I need her to know that I never stopped loving her. This call isn't to ask her to wait for me. I just need to know that she's okay."

There was a long pause on the other end of the line.

"We haven't heard from you in years... Lana thought you were dead."

"I made a big mistake, and I disappointed your daughter."

I don't think either of us knew what to say. I could sense her discomfort.

"I'll let her know you called."

***

The sun had just begun to set as we drove to a secure tarmac where the Con Air plane waited to transport us to our next holding facility. Here we go again with the whole big song and dance.

I shuffled down the aisle to my designated seat at the back of the plane. On my way, I noticed today's flight was coed. I felt terrible for these women.

If being a prisoner as a man was awful, then being a prisoner as a woman was a genuine hardship. The seat was located right between the engine and the bathroom. It was covered in duct tape. I knew I had arrived. I sat down and looked up at the heavens.

I got the message, God! Loud and clear!

Once again, the engines lulled me to sleep as we took off. Maybe falling asleep in those situations was my way of dealing with the stress, although my dreams had begun to haunt me more than my reality.

I awoke to the sound of crying. A young female inmate begged the marshals to please undo one handcuff to allow her to use the bathroom. They refused.

Let me describe the restraints placed on inmates during Con Air transit. First, you're in the least fashionable onesie on the market that buttons straight up the middle. Next, your ankles have shackles connected by a chain that comes up towards the center of your stomach, then around your waist, bound together with handcuffs in the middle. Finally, you have a blue box placed over your handcuffs to cover the access points to the interworking of the cuffs and prevent an escape. This outfit would give Harry Houdini a run for his money.

The young female inmate continued to scream for mercy. At last, I watched the marshals push the girl toward the bathroom near the rear of the plane. By the time she reached the door, it was too late. She had already gone in her pants. In a rage, the marshals shoved her into the lavatory. She melted with embarrassment. I couldn't help but think of Lenny all those years ago in Glen Mills. The pain and humiliation he endured were mirrored in that poor girl's face. The people and places may change, but the system and its methods never do.

The marshals cussed and screamed as they cleaned her, wrapped her in towels, put her into a plastic jumpsuit, and took her back to her seat. We were given a small bottle of water and crackers to distract us from the human rights violation taking place in the back of the plane.

I don't want to die on this plane.

That feeling left an imprint that still disturbs me to this day. Something about being handcuffed in an airplane 40,000 feet in the air is one of the most fucked up experiences you can ever have. I want to die on my terms. I could accept the idea of dying, but I couldn't accept the idea of dying in handcuffs.

***

Hours later, we landed somewhere in Pennsylvania. The marshals shuffled us off the plane and onto a bus. We drove through old warehouses and abandoned buildings. Eventually, the wastelands turned into farmlands as we arrived at Lewisburg Penitentiary.

November 15, 1932, was the first time inmates were housed there. I now stood outside the first penitentiary built by the BOP (Bureau of Prisons). It felt like I was walking back in time. A giant square-shaped white wall stood fifty yards from the main structure and surrounded the entire prison. Armed guards in gun towers overhead coddled rifles across their chests.

Walking through the prison doors, I imagined all the inmates who walked this path before me. I wondered how many never walked back out.

The guard opened a heavy metal door painted in pure lead. Its bottom corner edge had dragged across the floor so many times that it had dug a line into the concrete that looked like fingernail marks of a hand fighting off a predator. I was taken down a few short stairs into a small holding cell. I ducked my head as I entered a dungeon made entirely of concrete. There was an eerie tone inside the cell. I sat waiting on a bench, shackled and dirty.

After some hours, we were taken through a brick and metal labyrinth to a holdover unit. As I entered the cramped area, I saw inmates doing pull-ups from pipes that ran the length of the ceiling. A single hallway was the decrepit backbone that held together a room full of triple-decker metal bunk beds filled with the stench of warm bodies.

Weeks later, word came down from top brass that we were going to be shipped out in the morning. That evening, I was solicited to join a car. The term "car" refers to a group of inmates that another inmate would align themselves with for the remainder of their sentence, like a gang.

Two large white boys the size of Nebraska and Arkansas escorted me to a private meeting where two of Hitler's best henchmen, Hermann Göring, and Heinrich Himmler, awaited me. A crowd of white inmates stood guard by the doorway as I entered.

Waves of intimidation crashed down on me with each step further into the cell as I traversed the Red Sea of antisemites. Once inside, a human barricade of Nazis blocked my exit.

A man spoke to me in a language I didn't understand.

"Wirst du mit anderen Rassen zusammenleben, wenn wir morgen abreisen?"

My face must have conveyed my lack of comprehension.

"He wants to know whether or not you will buck tomorrow," said one of the Nazis.

"Buck" meant that I would refuse to live with anyone who wasn't white when we arrived at the next prison.

I leaned forward, looked around the room, and chose my words carefully.

"I grew up in Philly, one of the biggest cities in the country. I'm a Jew. I have no beef with the Blacks, Latinos, Asians, or anyone else."

To take that position at the beginning of my prison term meant the Nazis could have made my life a living hell for the duration of my stay. This choice would follow me like a shadow across the Federal system, no matter which prison I was shipped to.

Unfortunately, there are rules in prison whether you like it or not, that you have to live by. They looked at me with disgust and asked if I was sure that this was what I wanted to do. I said yes. I didn't understand their comments as I made my way out of the cell. It all sounded like German to me.

Of the few guys who decided to join that car, every last one of them was beaten, stabbed, or sexually assaulted at some point due to the rules that were enforced by the white supremacist gangs.

That night, I slept with one eye open as I waited for the morning to go back into transit. I was anxious about starting over at a new prison, but only one thing would fix that. Time.

***

This is a pre-paid call from an inmate at a Federal prison. Press one to accept.

Regardless of how long it had been, I skipped greetings with Mike and got straight to the point.

"Any luck?" I said.

Translation: *Did you find DaVinci?*

"Yes and no. I spoke to the management in her building. I gave them her name. I even gave them Mona's nickname. They denied ever having any resident by that name," Mike said.

Translation: *I went to DaVinci's condo and asked for him by his real name and his nickname. No one knew who I was talking about.*

"Fuck!"

Translation: *I'm fucked.*

"After that, I called all the family members from your phone book. Most of them hung up on me. The rest said they hadn't heard from her, and one of her relatives asked me if I was looking for a job," Mike said.

Translation: *Most of your contacts wouldn't speak with me, and no one had seen DaVinci. The last one was either trying to recruit me or rob me.*

"Last time I saw him, we took a trip to the desert to meet the steakhouse guy. Then he pulled a Houdini on me."

Translation: *We were in Las Vegas to meet the Texas plug when he went missing.*

"So what's next? What do I do? Head to the steakhouse or stay vegetarian?" Mike asked.

Translation: *Do I go to Texas or stay in Philly?*

"The rabbit doesn't run this race. The turtle does while he sits this one out. Get Magnum to binocular it. Give him the car on the side of the road and the name of the interstate."

Translation: *Stay in Philly. Hire a private investigator and have him look into it. Give him the breakdown of where I last saw DaVinci.*

"A President's relationship to money," Mike said and ended our call.

Translation: *I'm on it.*

24.

I arrived at my destination the following afternoon. It was a medium/high-security prison in upstate New York. When I stepped off the bus, insects swarmed me in the burning August heat. The prison was called Ray Brook. I was told that I would be staying there for three weeks. I ended up staying for three years.

Ray Brook was initially built as an athletic training facility for the 1980 Olympics and designed to be converted into a prison after the games. Located atop a hill sat five individual cell blocks. The yard, chow hall, and commissary were all located on the lower level of the compound. Ray Brook had a notorious reputation for being a harsh prison in a freezing environment. Both inside, and out.

The sun blinded me when I stepped out onto the compound. I heard a fox cry off in the distance somewhere, or at least I thought I did. My bedding and supplies were folded across both of my arms. I was dirty and tired, wearing that awful orange jumper and navy blue Bruce Lee slippers.

I got the message, God! Loud and clear!

I stood still and waited for my eyes to adjust to the blinding sunlight. Only to see a vast open compound with no one in sight. Just me, confusion, a guard station, tan brick buildings, and fences wrapped with more barbed wire than a pair of biceps in a bad 1990s movie.

When you're lost in prison, it's not like being lost in a city as a tourist. If you stop to ask for help from a CO the typical response you get is *you better hurry the fuck up and figure it out*. This was the white glove treatment compared to rubber bullets and mace.

I was excited about change, but change came with the hardship of the unknown. You must find a new pillow, food, chair, blanket, supplies, mattress, and cell. This part I hated.

Niagara B unit sat on a hill in the back left corner of the compound. I heard only my footsteps as I walked across the yard to get there. Row after row of cell windows looked upon me. I couldn't see a single face, but it felt like all eyes were on me.

When I entered the unit, a group of inmates began to question me.

"Where are you from?"

"Philly."

"What are you in for?"

"Conspiracy to commit drug trafficking."

"How long did you get?"

"110 months."

"You did good."

"What?" I said.

"Do you need anything?"

"No."

"Have you found Jesus?"

"Yes, but his name is pronounced *Jesús,* and he's from the Dominican Republic, serving fifteen years for cocaine trafficking. He came in on the bus with me this morning."

Unfazed by my remark, an inmate handed me a Bible.

"Save yourself."

I was designated to live in a ten-man cell with one toilet and a neighbor three feet away on either side of me. If you complained about living in a ten-man cell, the COs would shakedown the cell to aggravate your cellmates and make you a target for retaliation. Over the years, many inmates and civil rights lawyers challenged the legitimacy of these cells in the courts because of the inhuman conditions. The way the hierarchy worked was that you would go from a ten-man to a six-man, to a four-man, and then a two-man cell if you could work your way up the ladder. I didn't want to do any of that. I wanted to skip the line and go straight to the top shelf.

My new cellmate was a gang member from California who'd been in prison since he was fifteen. I provided him with paperwork to prove I wasn't an informant or a sex offender so I could move into his two-man cell. Grateful to go from nine roommates to one, I gifted him that Bible given to me as a token of appreciation.

This was the first time I relaxed a little in the last two and a half years. Yes, he was a two-time convicted murderer, but somehow light-hearted, funny, and a pretty nice guy. Imagine a man who started doing push-ups and just never stopped. That was him. We were cellmates for a year before he went to the hole for getting caught with a knife. Hidden ironically in that same Bible. Did I mention he was in for double murder?

The average inmate in Ray Brook was serving thirty years. I was the odd man out. Now I understood what that inmate meant when he said *you did good*. The reason I was being held in a medium-security prison was due to an open warrant from that day in Philly when I saved DaVinci. My unresolved case caused my custody classification points to increase. Legally, I could be kept in a medium prison as long as I had that open warrant. If I were to win at trial or have the case in Philly dismissed, I'd be eligible to serve my time in a low-security prison or a satellite camp with no fences and more liberties. That is where I should've been sent initially based on the nature of my offense and having no convictions on my criminal record.

It amazed me to think about how my choices that day in Philadelphia continued to affect the quality of my life in Federal prison. I regretted my poor decisions, but on that day, with the circumstances at hand, I wouldn't have changed a thing. My loyalty to DaVinci meant everything to me.

I have to get out of here.

To light a fire under the District Attorney's ass in Philly, I filed The Right To A Speedy Trial Act. They had one hundred eighty days to get me to trial or dismiss my charge. My case did not carry steep penalties in the State. If Philadelphia found me guilty, my sentence would run concurrent rather than consecutive, meaning I would serve the state time parallel to my Federal time. Win or lose. It made no difference. I was going to trial.

25.

The dreaded great white prison bus. The same one I caught glimpses of when I was a child as it swam in and out of the city streets just off the shore of the Delaware River. That metal monster had me clutched in its teeth as it pulled me down toward the center of the city. I admired the beautiful architecture of our nation's once-grand capital. History and culture blended on the canvas of America to form a unique pastel, the hue of a junkie. Nothing screams freedom like watching a vagabond urinate fifty feet from where the Liberty Bell sits.

I arrived downtown before the courts opened, and was given a brief phone call to my court-appointed attorney before going to trial.

"Stein, Steinman, and Steinman-stein, how may I help you?"

"Good morning. I'm trying to contact the worst lawyer on earth."

"Connecting you now with public defender Lisa Patel. Please hold."

After a few minutes on hold, she answered.

"Lisa Patel speaking."

"Hi, Lisa. You told me to call you when I came down from New York Federal prison. Do you remember the car chase case?"

"Yes, would you like to plead guilty or extra guilty?"

In all seriousness, I was not going to plead guilty. I intended to go to trial. I had been running to evade a conviction since this case started. Why stop now?

The courtroom interior matched the outside of the courthouse: cold, numb, and grey. I sat down in the defendant's chair, where my assigned counsel, Mrs. Patel, awaited me. When the judge entered the courtroom, I stood and faced the jury. My public defender leaned over and murmured, "I hope this goes well."

The judge shuffled a few papers, whispered some comments to the clerk nearest him, and looked up at us.

"Let the prosecution call their first witness."

Even if it was brief, that high-speed chase left me fighting about fifteen charges. It'd been years since the alleged incident. The hope for the best today would be expecting the worst. The prosecution's only witness was the same cop who arrested me that day when I ran from the car to save DaVinci.

The cop took the stand and began to testify in great detail about what had occurred during the alleged car chase, except for the part where they beat me up after they arrested me. I sat helplessly, listening to the officer's testimony. This wasn't going well for me. He stated that we took off down an alleyway when he attempted to stop the vehicle for a traffic violation. When he got to the part about DaVinci, he stated that the driver fled left as a Latino-looking suspect fled from the rear passenger side with what appeared to be a red duffle bag toward the right. He continued until the point where they cuffed me.

"Is the man sitting in the defendant's chair the driver of the vehicle that engaged in a high-speed chase with the police?" the prosecutor asked.

A man wearing a navy blue suit came in from the back of the courtroom, walked toward me, and shook my hand.

"A friend sent me," he said.

The officer stopped his testimony as the judge paused momentarily to speak with Mrs. Patel and the man in the navy suit, who seemed to be my new lawyer. The lawyers took their seats on either side of me, and the judge asked the prosecution to please continue.

"Officer, once again, is the man sitting in the defendant's chair the driver of the vehicle who engaged in a high-speed chase with the police?"

Every muscle in my body tensed up. I looked the police officer right in his eyes. He looked back at me and contemplated. His response came out in awkward pieces.

"I... ah... can't say... if that's him... or not."

I want to say that I celebrated at that moment, but I was so confused that I didn't realize that the witness's inability to identify me meant that I had most likely won the case. The prosecution followed up with a few more cursory questions before turning the witness over to the defense.

The man in the navy suit stood, adjusted his tie, cleared his throat, and said, "Thank you, Your Honor. I have no further questions."

He turned to me and shook my hand.

"Have a nice day."

What the fuck?

The man in the navy suit walked out of the courtroom before the judge banged the gavel. I was expecting half of the 15th District to be there that day, along with multiple detailed reports and evidence of my fingerprints all over the steering wheel. To this day, I still have no idea who the man in the navy suit was nor who had sent him.

The judge looked at the prosecutor, Mrs. Patel, and then at me. Full of frustration, he yelled at the prosecution.

"You guys never cease to amaze me. You leave me with no choice. Case dismissed."

***

I savored my courtroom victory as we drove up State Road along the Delaware River back to the Curran-Fromhold Correctional Facility, known as CFCF. CFCF was a transit stop and county jail where inmates were held before being rerouted to another prison. CFCF was named after the two wardens killed in Holmesburg Prison on May 31, 1973.

When I was a free man, two things always left me in awe when I used to drive down Torresdale Avenue past Rhawn Street. The fantastic colors of trees during fall in Pennypack Park and the iconic cut of the stones that made up the wall that surrounded Holmesburg prison.

I was stunned when I walked through that dinosaur's hallways. To touch its bones was more of an experience than a punishment. This prison was closed in 1995, but because the prison population on State Road was so high, they started housing inmates in Holmesburg Prison again.

Upon return, a group of correctional officers in tactical riot gear gathered to search us. They were overzealous, overly aggressive, but more importantly, overdressed. The senior officer of the crowd yelled, "Fellas, listen up! As we go down the line, loudly state your name, strip, turn around, squat, and cough, then get dressed. Pay attention!"

The first inmate yelled, "Harris, Tyrone," turned, squatted, and coughed.

The second inmate yelled, "Nguyen, Trang," turned, squatted, and coughed.

The third inmate yelled, "Gomez, Jose," turned, squatted, and coughed.

They approached me next. In my best Sean Connery James Bond, I yelled out, "*The name'sh Naked. Buck Naked.*"

Some of the inmates burst into laughter. Perhaps my victory at trial had given me a little too much confidence. The officer closest to me went ballistic and jumped in my face. He sucker-punched me hard in the gut. Not ready for the blow to my solar plexus, I folded over.

"Do we have a fucking problem!" the CO screamed.

Catching my breath I said, "Nope. No problem here."

***

After the trial, the state authorities failed to transfer me back to Federal custody. Poor communication from both parties left me to rot in that Philadelphia holding facility indefinitely. I figured I'd get my bail money refunded and a copy of my court transcripts from the trial before I returned to Ray Brook. I called my attorney to ask for assistance in gathering my paperwork.

"Hi Lisa, this is the guy who won the car chase case."

"What can I do for you?"

"I need my court transcripts before I return to Federal prison."

"I'm not sure how I can help you. After you win, I'm no longer your attorney."

"No, no, no, unlike me, you're not getting off that easy. I need my paperwork please."

Rejoining the Federal prison population wouldn't be possible without the necessary paperwork to explain to my fellow inmates why I went back to court.

Often, if an inmate goes back to court while serving their sentence, it's to cooperate with the government to reduce their time. If you did not have an appeal in the courts pending, and your sentence was reduced, your release date would change, proving that you cooperated. People get killed over that.

If inmates even thought you testified, it wouldn't be good for you. Once you're labeled a rat, you'll wear that Chucky Cheese birthday hat forever. That hat is known as a buck fifty, as it takes roughly 150 stitches to seal your injuries after you get slashed in the face.

I resolved my case and recouped my bail. It was time to return to Ray Brook. I spent six months at CFCF before being shipped back to Federal prison. If I had never spoken up, I'd probably still be there right now.

*****

I applied for a transfer the day that I returned to Ray Brook. Since I had completed all of the necessary legal requirements I believed the prison would now comply and approve my transfer. I was wrong.

Management variables are used depending on each inmate's security needs. They are based on your history of violence, age, and the length of your sentence. A management variable could stipulate the condition for a higher or lower- security prison. As a camp custody inmate, I was no longer supposed to live with or interact with medium-custody inmates. When my custody points were reevaluated, I was sent to live in a work cadre unit. Still, on the same compound with zero separation from the medium custody inmates.

Shortly after my return, the inmates from Philadelphia requested that I come down to the prison yard with my paperwork. Prison politics require that if you are requested down to the yard, you go. If you don't, you've made yourself a target.

The moment I walked into the yard, the inmates from Philly surrounded me. One of the inmates knew me from the street. He began to recite my full legal name, inmate number, and the Philadelphia case number for my trial.

"I know who you are," he said.

A bit shocked by the accuracy of his information I was more relieved than ever that I didn't leave Philly without my legal paperwork. I handed my documents over to him.

The last time he saw me I was a muscular 220 pounds, but years passed and prison involuntarily starved me down to a slim 180. I still had heart, but now was a mere shadow of the man I once was when on the streets of Philadelphia. He couldn't conceal his surprise.

"What the fuck happened to you? How did you end up here?"

"Well, I went to see my doctor. He said, 'I'm sorry, I've got some bad news for you. You're getting indicted'."

I asked him what should I do.

He handed me a box of bullets and said, "Take two, and don't call me in the morning."

26.

The first thing I noticed in Ray Brook was the chilling silence. The only sound I ever heard was the ambient background noise of human suffering. The TV's volume is broadcast through AM/FM radio stations, which inmates listen to with headphones. There's one TV for each race to help keep the fights to a minimum. If you run a TV, and someone tries to change the channel, no questions asked, you have to fight them on the spot.

When the hope of going to another prison flatlined, I felt stuck inside the movie *Groundhog Day*. I watched the same shitty cable, every same shitty day, every same shitty year, and no matter how many shows I watched, it was always the same story. Overdosing on boredom, I pried off the syringe cap, unscrewed the Narcan capsule, and let her rip. Bing! I had an epiphany.

I knew I would have to find a hustle to get any of the limited luxuries available in prison. Prisoners used a primitive economy to allow transactions to take place. A monetary system built on packages of tuna and postal stamps. I used this Stone Age system to build a castle behind those walls.

One cigarette in prison sold for twenty dollars apiece. Twenty in a pack, ten packs in a carton. The juice was worth the squeeze. I found a way to make money without being directly involved. If it looks like a duck, walks like a duck, and quacks like a duck, it's probably a criminal.

Over the next few years, I acquired several new amenities. My acquisitions included an office chair, the swiveling kind, a stainless steel toilet with a matching range made from two irons to make paninis, a microwave, and a bed the size of a loveseat. I also had two triple-stuffed feather pillows and a blacklight I appropriated from the kitchen made from Italian bug zappers. However, my prize acquisition was a color TV with full sound.

Inmates maintain everything in prison, including TV replacement and repairs. I paid an inmate repairman three cigarettes to install a TV with speakers and a kill switch for the volume. I had my very own private TV in a small TV room. My eardrums were in love with the sound coming from that old, dirty, outdated television. I fell asleep every night to the sound of Turner Classic Movies.

I developed a romantic attachment to the world of cinema. It was my freedom. It was my escape. I wasn't just watching a movie. I projected myself into another life, another me. The characters weren't just fiction. They were the small pieces of my imagination that I allowed myself to explore. I was able to dream beyond the reality of my surroundings. Those characters reflected the one thing that I wanted but couldn't buy in prison. Singularity in a plural world.

***

This is a pre-paid call from an inmate at a Federal prison. Press one to accept.

"Mike, tell me you found the missing child on the side of the milk box."

Translation: *Tell me you found Da Vinci.*

"Depends how you view it. Which do you want first, the wedding or the funeral?" Mike asked.

Translation: *I've got good news, and I've got bad news.*

"Hit me."

Translation: *Give me the bad news.*

"The guy I hired to look for the painter found a movie starring a guy he thought was him. The second letter and fifth letter. Elvis has left the building," Mike said.

Translation: *The investigator found him or at least someone he thought was Da Vinci. The second letter was B, for breaking. The fifth letter was E, for entering. He acquired security footage of a man going into Da Vinci's high-rise, exiting down a stairwell, and out the back door of the building.*

"A man drives in circles. I refuse to let my wife ask for directions."

Translation: *I'm lost.*

Mike repeated his translation in code.

"The Renaissance guy wasn't in the film. There was some breaking and some entering by a phantom who floated out the back," Mike said.

"I'm still in the car Mike, help me out?"

Translation: *I'm lost. I'm not following.*

Mike repeated his translation in code.

"Mona and Lisa were nowhere to be found. They're gone, moved, disappeared. I don't fucking know. There's a video of a guy eating at an In-and- Out Burger. Then he vanishes."

I grew irritated, not understanding what he was saying. I yelled, "Just give it to me straight, man!"

Translation: *Stop talking in code. I'm fucking lost.*

"The investigator said no one by the name of DaVinci or anyone by DaVinci's legal name has ever lived at that address. He has security footage of the man who broke into the condo. He asked if I recognized the guy in the video. I said no, but I recognized the blurry face. He wanted to contact the police because he felt that foul play may have been involved," Mike said.

"So what about the guy in the video?" I asked.

"Well, that's the thing. Are you sure you want me to say it?"

"Yes, just fucking say it," I said.

"It's not DaVinci in the video... it's you."

"Zeros and ones! Zeros and ones!" I exclaimed.

Translation: *Abort. Go back to code*!

"Pizza and platinum," Mike said.

Translation: *The day you broke into DaVinci's.*

"Leave it alone. The last thing I need is another unexplained charge on my credit card bill. I fucking hate I can't figure out that wanted poster," I said.

Translation: *I don't want to get charged with another crime, but I hate not knowing if he's dead or alive.*

"Just let it go then. The painter is gone. Keep your head up. At least you're still here, even if it's not in the best place," Mike said.

Paranoid and defeated, I knew he was right, but I still couldn't come to terms with reality.

"Love you, Mike. See you on the other side."

***

Even though I lived comfortably at Ray Brook, I still wanted out. A medium- security prison environment is as dangerous as a balancing act on a tightrope high above a war zone. Twenty-four-seven, three sixty-five, and even while I slept, I was awake.

To deter me from utilizing my legal right to file a grievance, they used stall tactics and denials, knowing it could take years to get to the court, and by the time my complaint was heard, it would be ruled moot because it was no longer relevant.

After years of lockdowns due to violence on the compound, I filed a grievance on record about being housed illegally there. In return, the staff painted a bullseye on my back. They felt I wasn't listening and increased the frequency of overall harassment to ensure I knew my place as a prisoner. Now a human target in Ray Brook, I was at the top of the endangered species list.

***

I didn't typically eat at the chow hall, but if I did go, it was to give my tray away to another inmate who needed food. Not all inmates had enough money on their books to afford commissary, nor the connections to acquire food by other means.

One evening, I arrived at the chow hall with my work gloves and chapstick in my pockets. When I sat down at the table, my buddy said to me, "Dude, if looks could kill, that CO just murdered you twice."

At the exit of the chow hall, a separate hallway passed by the lieutenant's office. A side door used only by staff connected the dining area to the front of the office.

"Let me know when the CO isn't looking," I said.

He kept watching. "Wait... wait... wait for it. Go!"

I was almost out of the chow hall when that same CO burst through the side door.

"Stop! Put your hands on the wall!"

He gave me a cursory pat down, squeezed my left pocket with the chapstick inside, and forced me into the lieutenant's office.

Within minutes, additional higher-ranking staff members appeared. It wasn't normal for a Lieutenant and a Captain to be present during a routine pat search. The fact that they had made an appearance on my behalf meant that something bad was about to happen. There's no such thing as a coincidence. The search was perfunctory. They had no interest in the contents of my pockets. All three backed me into a small cell and stood in the doorway.

"Take off your clothes! Now!" the Lieutenant shouted.

"I don't have anything."

I stood in my boxers as they screamed in my face for me to strip while inmates passed the office window. The CO stood on my right, the Lieutenant was in the middle, and the Captain stood on my left.

I snapped, "I'm not stripping nude in front of the whole fucking compound!"

"Strip! Now! The windows are two-way mirrors," the Lieutenant said.

I had passed those windows for years. I knew they were only active with the sun's reflection on them during the day, but they didn't function at night.

"The fuck they are!" I yelled.

A gauge of the absolute differential between us pressured me to comply. Reluctantly, I dropped my drawers but covered my genitals.

"Let go! Move your hand!" the Captain screamed.

"Is this what you want? What the fuck!" I snapped.

The CO approached me with gloves.

"Open your mouth. Stick out your tongue. Move it around. Turn your head. Show me behind each ear. Shake your hair. Lift your balls. Turn around. Lift each foot. Pull your cheeks open. Squat and cough."

Through physiological humiliation, they wished to break me psychologically. It's an ancient tactic. The mind and body are a delicate balance.

"You're not supposed to have chapstick on the compound," the

Lieutenant said as I got dressed.

"They sell it on commissary," I responded.

The CO broke the tube in half in hopes of finding contraband inside. They couldn't bust me for chapstick and found no contraband to justify their strip search. The Lieutenant picked up the work gloves.

"These gloves aren't inmate-issued."

"I work outside, and my job issued them to me."

"You're not supposed to bring them inside of the prison. You forget about what happened here, and we'll forget about the gloves."

I was the prisoner, and they were the guards. That's the way it was. I left the Lieutenant's office and went back to my cell.

***

It was a cold and foggy morning when I left Ray Brook. By the grace of God, my new caseworker finally acknowledged my grievance and processed my transfer. Handcuffed, shackled, and wearing only a thin jumpsuit, every breath lingered in the air. The bus rumbled to life as the driver with a mid-section as round as his steering wheel fired up the engine. I leaned my head against the window, but it was difficult to find sleep with my neck in an awkward position. A voice came over the loudspeaker and boomed throughout the bus.

Good morning, gentlemen. Today's ride will be approximately two hours, so sit back, relax in your shackles, and enjoy the worst bus ride of your life. Please remember, if you try to escape, we will shoot your ass. We're not going for any of that Richard Kimble bullshit. As far as we're concerned, you all killed your w ives.

I had spent the last three years in Ray Brook and had very little to show for it. The memories and experiences I had there were nothing more than shadows in the hallways of an emotionless institution. But I was no prisoner of a physical structure. I was a prisoner of time. Time had become a meaningless cycle of pain rather than a continuous joyful sensation.

The irony of my punishment is that I was sentenced to time for selling drugs, yet time itself behaves like a drug. Do enough of it, and it'll kill you.

27.

"I've got my eye on you."

These were the first words I heard when I stepped off the bus at Lewisburg prison camp. I had been transferred to the satellite camp attached to the main penitentiary building where I had been housed three years prior. The man who spoke those words to me was a corrections officer. He glared at me with piercing squinty eyes as I stood in line outside of the bus waiting to be unshackled. I noticed his high-water pants and coffee-stained shirt tightly tucked in over his pot belly.

Alongside me was another inmate I had met during a holdover at FCI Canaan who was serving time for marijuana trafficking. He asked me how old I was and how long I had been in prison. We were the same age, and he was serving a sentence approximately half the length of mine.

"That was your whole twenties," he said. "I only lost half of mine. So many years of so many young men's lives have been wasted."

I didn't know what to make of it, but I could see that he was taken aback. I believed that he was having a moment of clarity regarding his own time in prison.

"Did you see that hallway?" he asked.

"It stretched into an eternity."

He was referring to the hallway in Canaan. It ran as far as the eye could see. A cold, clinical corridor that had doors along one side to allow bodies to be housed in the most efficient way possible. The architecture was surgical. It had no end, and it had no beginning. It was limbo.

We left Canaan and were sent to Lewisburg to serve the remainder of our time together. He spent his days studying language and writing screenplays. He would eventually become the person who helped me write the book you're reading right now.

For the first time in years, I stood semi-free outside a secure facility with no fences, handcuffs, or shackles. My first instinct was to run. Therein lies the insult. You can't run. Even if I were to wait until the middle of the night, sprint to a getaway car, obtain a fake passport, and abscond to Thailand, I would eventually be apprehended and sent back to the United States to serve even more time in a higher security prison. The power of the FBI is limitless. They will always find you. Doing time in a camp with no fences is staring freedom in the face and crawling back to your cell every night. Federal prison camps with no fences are a cold statement on the nature of compliance.

I was processed through intake, given clothes, and then sent down to meet my case manager. Ignoring his theatrics, and false gestured formalities, I requested to see my jacket.

He stuttered, "Wha, well, why do you want to see that?"

My case manager knew exactly why I wanted to see my jacket. I learned that information protected me, not only from the inmates but from the staff as well. The form I requested within my jacket was an unofficial list of who gets special disciplinary treatment.

"Don't worry about your jacket. If we want you gone, you're gone," he said.

***

RDAP is a nine-month residential drug abuse program. In Federal prison, RDAP is a way to reduce time off of your sentence. It is the only way to reduce time off of your sentence aside from a fifty-four-day yearly reduction, which is given to inmates based on good behavior. On average, most inmates released without completing RDAP receive three to four months in a halfway house. RDAP guarantees a full six months in a halfway house as well as three to twelve months of a potential reduction of your sentence.

Let's be clear. Whether you're serving three years or thirty years, RDAP is the only way to reduce the length of your sentence without cooperating with the government, and the total length in reduction is no more than twelve months. This was a highly desirable program for every eligible inmate. Was I a junkie? No, but my lawyer said I had better pretend to be one if I wanted to get out early.

The RDAP unit consisted of two large rooms with bunks scattered throughout them. Active participants were housed on the right side, and those waiting to join the program were housed on the left. Two hundred and forty beds, six toilets, six urinals, and twelve showers. To put it lightly, the living environment was unsanitary.

While I waited for the program, I focused on training and furthering my education. I created a workout called Form, Breathing, and Technique. It's a method of using flawless form throughout your movements to maximize your caloric expenditure. I taught my regimen for free to anyone who wanted to better their health. To quote Bruce Lee, "Empty your mind, be formless. Shapeless, like water."

Time flew by as I stayed busy with my routine, but boredom made me see the loopholes in the camp, so I couldn't help but begin to jump through them. Lewisburg was a labor camp that hosted an electronics recycling facility called Unicore. The existence of Unicore lent itself to the availability of a variety of electronic devices. Coupled with a fenceless compound, you could see how Lewisburg became the Walmart of contraband— K2, weed, liquor, drugs, cigarettes, cell phones, and even hookers. *Talk about going the extra mile to get laid.*

I was hired to work in the Fire Safety Equipment Department, managing fire extinguishers and recycling for the compound. It had a few perks and zero oversight. The first perk was that my job required me to drive around the prison compound to perform my duties. Sometimes, it was a van or truck, but I most often drove a golf cart. Its short battery life, terrible paint job, and rust orange finish had me going zero to nowhere in sixty minutes. As guys waited in line for the chow hall, I'd zip by them, double park, and stroll right in. Inmates would ask me, "How the fuck are you getting away with this?"

"Simple, I work in safety. Is everyone safe? Do you guys feel safe?"

They looked at me incredulously.

"No, we don't," they replied.

"Great! Then I still have a job."

Most of my afternoons were spent outdoors in a dusty workspace about half the size of a tennis court adjacent to the Unicore warehouse. Logistically, it gave me access to the entire prison, which helped me acquire different materials to cover up the high fence that surrounded my workspace. Green tarps used to cover up freight containers were perfect for cutting down the wind inside the fenced area. And well, let's just say one thing led to another, and it might've gotten out of hand.

We had a roof, so all I needed to do was add walls. Over a period of months, I used a forklift to hoist the green tarps up one piece at a time and secure it from the top of the fence down to the floor. Hard work was made even more difficult in the brutally cold weather, but I suffered through it. This might not seem like much, but I was eroding the shoreline of the prison and building a beachfront paradise.

Because of the tarps that I had hung around the workspace, we were no longer visible to the outside compound, and with no one to stop me, I got to work— on building my apartment.

For the inside walls, I used one-ton capacity cardboard boxes from the recycling facility. I unraveled, soaked, and then hung them out to dry. These giant sheets of cardboard transformed into homemade drywall. I built a room inside the covered work area. It was a small room with no door. The interior consisted of a single bunk, desk, radio, and microwave. You know, the standard minimal furnishings for any illegal apartment in prison.

After all my hard work at not working, I could do nothing but sleep in peace. The only thing that sucked was that my feet were still freezing. So

I got a small space heater, kicked my shoes off, and roasted my feet at the end of the bed. Ah, life couldn't get any better, or could it? It could.

I built a small kitchen to add to my tiny apartment. Pots and pans hung above dual hot plates on countertops. To have a setup like this was phenomenal but, more importantly, impossible.

This exclusive beachfront property was known as Hell's Kitchen. A former New York City firefighter nicknamed "Pat The Bat" happened to be an excellent chef and created pure art with pasta and meatballs made from scratch. We spent countless afternoons huddled in the kitchen, enjoying the fruits of his labor. Pat was wrongfully convicted of a marijuana conspiracy charge and was later exonerated after spending three years in Federal prison.

With all the new renovations, my co-workers grew increasingly worried about what would happen if the staff learned about our exclusive property. If it went bust, I'd step up to take the blame. I didn't want anyone to get in trouble over my actions. While it sounds like a summer camp, remember, I was still very much in Federal prison. The penalties to be paid if I were caught ranged from severe to possibly being charged with a crime.

Shortly after I started the RDAP program, I realized how bad it was to sleep inside the unit, which was constructed of aluminum and had no insulation. It was freezing in the winter, and in the summer, it reached over a hundred degrees in the building. We were given fans by the staff to distribute throughout the unit near our bunks. However, for the size of the building, we weren't given nearly enough to go around.

To help beat the heat, I stole every fan on the compound that wasn't tied down and brought them back to our unit. One fan was located in an old wooden shed on a remote part of the compound. Another inmate and I worked together to remove the fan that hung from the ceiling. The other inmate flipped the breaker on at the exact moment that I was detaching the wires. An electric charge exploded from the wires and shot a bolt of fire across the ceiling. I grabbed a nearby fire extinguisher and attempted to put the fire out. It was empty. I chucked it aside and we began beating the flames out with our khaki shirts. Afterward, I examined the tag of the empty fire extinguisher. Of course, my signature was on the certification tag. Perhaps I should have been paying a little more attention to my duties at the Fire Safety Equipment Department.

***

The final year of my sentence came faster than expected, and that same CO who first took notice of me when I stepped off the bus upon my arrival at Lewisburg was still gunning for me. Ray Brook was a permanent jacket that I wore whether I liked it or not. Harassment is the price I paid for breaking the rules.

It was the night before Christmas when staff lost complete control over the inmates. It was discovered that prostitutes were on the compound during the wee hours of the night. What can I say? The Dominicans had their ways. The compound was raided by an exterior task force, and the inmates were placed on lockdown. However, our primary punishment was not the lockdown. It was the removal of the TVs and microwaves.

To keep the Christmas spirit alive, I smuggled a microwave into the housing unit and stashed it under a bunk in the back. One by one, inmates came hat in hand to use it. We huddled around the microwave like children around an evergreen tree on Christmas morning. With some assistance from one of Santa's little helpers, otherwise known as *Jesús*, the cocaine trafficker from the Dominican Republic who for some odd reason I seemed unable to escape, helped hand out one hundred McDonald's cheeseburgers. That one-dollar cheeseburger tasted not only like a million bucks, but freedom. The spirit of Christmas was alive, and it was the breadline to a prisoner's soul.

***

Every Wednesday and Saturday after lunch, I took a solo jog around the compound to clear my mind. The breeze cooled my skin, and the natural high lifted my feet from the ground. In the distance, another runner was coming into sight. As he neared me, I realized it was a panicked co-worker.

"They found Hell's Kitchen! The guards want us up at the workspace now!"

"I'll shower and come up. Tell the guys I'll take full responsibility," I said.

My fellow inmates depended on me to keep my word, and I knew if I was detained, it might be days before I'd see a shower again. So I packed my things in preparation to be locked up and headed up to the Fire Safety Equipment Department.

The guards stood waiting for me as I entered the apartment that had stood in plain sight, unbeknownst to them for over a year. I was unsure what to expect but was prepared for the consequences. Furiously, one CO shouted, "What the fuck is going on out here!"

"It's freezing out here and we are the only job without cover. I used tarps to stop the winds from cutting through my bones," I said.

"And what about the rest of this fucking shit? It looks like a homeless encampment."

Personally, I thought it resembled more of a home in Kensington, Philadelphia, but now wasn't the time to argue property values in Pennsylvania.

"It was all stuff that was just lying around. I was merely keeping the place organized," I said.

"Finish your fucking work and go back to your units. We'll talk more about this tomorrow."

That night, back at the unit, I assured everyone that I would dive onto the grenade. The other inmates agreed that no one would tell staff how it was built. That's all I needed to hear, and I knew I had a shot at not getting in trouble if I handled it. I accepted whatever might happen tomorrow, but my punishment never got that far.

The guards sealed off Hell's Kitchen, evicted the tenants, and stripped the apartment of its amenities. Somehow, impossibly, that was all that came of it. I'd realize later that I had probably gotten away with it because if the staff had reported the incident to higher-ups, they would have indirectly made themselves look incompetent.

When I began serving my prison sentence, I mentioned that I would make a strong effort not to become institutionalized. Rather than allowing the institutions to modify my lifestyle in order to fit into their structures, I managed to modify their structures to fit into my lifestyle. Between the private TV at Ray Brook and the beachfront apartment at Lewisburg, I believe I succeeded.

***

From the beginning of my incarceration, I was haunted by the memory of her. I'd wake up physically ill and try to shake off the pain of a lost love. Year after year, I called, and year after year, no one answered. Dreams of her laying in my arms, wrapped up next to me, lingered well after I opened my eyes to the reality of my daily life in prison. I can't say that I was the only one. I'm sure countless men carried the pain of unrequited love through the corridors of incarceration. I could never shake the sound of her heartbeat, no matter how faint it grew. More than the hope of freedom, it was the hope of hearing her voice one last time that kept me alive.

This is a pre-paid call from an inmate at a Federal prison. Press one to accept.

"Hello."

The sound of Lana's voice melted through the prison phone line.

"I'm surprised to hear from you," she said.

"You're my first love and best friend. Lana, of course, I was going to call."

"Wow, how long has it been?" she asked.

"Almost a decade."

"Are you okay in there?"

"Well, that depends on how well you can live in hell."

She laughed.

"When are you coming home?"

"When that door hits me in the ass. I could be out soon, but I'll never truly be free until I let go of all this."

"Don't talk like that. You'll make it. If anyone can get out of there, it's you."

"Do you still have the lyrical poem I wrote for you?"

"Yes."

"And the record player?"

"Yes. I love that record player. I still use it."

The record player was the only piece of my childhood that remained. A gift from my dad that carried with it a sense of innocence that had long since faded away.

"I'm sorry. I should have visited or written, but I didn't know how to tell you," she said.

"Tell me what?" But I already knew.

"I'm married," she paused. "I don't know how to say it..."

"Lana, you can tell me anything."

"... I'm pregnant."

Hearing those words hurt, still not as much as the years I'd spent away from her. I knew once the handcuffs hit my wrists that our life together was over.

"Do you love him?"

Lana was quiet. I didn't ask her to compare myself to him. I asked because I genuinely wanted her to be happy.

"You disappeared," she said, "I wanted to marry you and have a child, but you chose that life."

"I know, Lana. You're right. It's my fault, I'm sorry, and I was wrong."

She began to cry.

"I knew you were gone, and I just couldn't," she said.

"You were the light at the end of my tunnel, but we were young, and sadly, life goes on. You're a wonderful woman, and I know you'll be an even more beautiful mother."

Through her tears, she said, "I love you, and I always will."

"Lana. That's why I never stopped calling. I love—"

Our call was disconnected. The allotted time per call had expired. The hope I had thrived on for nearly a decade was gone. Lana was a memory. A relic from my former life that died alongside the years of my youth that I had wasted in a world of crime and incarceration.

***

New Year's Eve was a reflection of the word "last." The next year would be the last time I would spend another holiday, birthday, or milestone in prison. The upcoming year wouldn't be just another one wasted. It was to be celebrated. I finally began to allow myself to think about the first thing I might do when I was released. Would I live in a house? What would I eat? Who would I see first? I could only imagine things that I had seen or done in the past. It was a difficult concept to wrap my head around. Memory works in mysterious ways.

***

We were seated in the morning RDAP meeting room, when twenty minutes into our session, four COs appeared and stood outside of the community room door. I thought they had finally decided to lock me up for Hell's Kitchen after all.

I looked past the rows of inmates and at the four COs in the hallway, one of them waved for me to come out to them. I played dumb, shrugged, and gave a hitchhiker's thumb to the guy on my left. Two COs shook their head no. I pointed to the guy on my right. Three COs shook their heads no. I pointed at myself. All four in a frustrated unison nodded their heads *yes*. The words from my case manager, when I arrived at the Lewisburg camp, replayed in my head. "*If we want you gone, you're gone.*"

Fuck it. I stood up, approached my friends, shook their hands, and said goodbye. I then said hello to a question that stood waiting for me in the hallway.

"Name and inmate number?" demanded the CO closest to me.

Verifying my government name and eight digits led me to be cuffed and escorted up the hill to the main prison building. The four COs boxed me in while two held my arms securely on each side.

"Third time's a charm," I said as I entered Lewisburg Penitentiary, wiping my feet on an intricately designed welcome mat made from decades of misery. They escorted me down to a cold, damp basement.

I was led to a cell suited for no one, not even an animal. It was a cage the size of a phone booth made of metal bars that ran from the ceiling to the floor. I was stripped naked and forced into a standing stress position for hours.

A long stairway to hell went up to Lewisburg's Special Management Unit

(SMU). I counted each step on my way up the dark stairwell. Slipping. Falling. I fell.

"Get the fuck up, inmate!" the CO yelled.

A hand reached out to help me up. "Stay close to me. I will show you a way forward."

I turned darkness into light and walked by faith, not sight. They led me through a metal gate down to the end of a hallway, inundated with bizarre cries from inmates behind locked doors. Cells like uniformed piano keys ran down each side of me— notes of abuse played behind the thick steel doors. I had no idea that a piece of Cuba existed on the on the third floor of the Lewisburg Penitentiary. Metal clanked on my body as I shuffled toward my cell. The key turned, a door opened, me in, arms out, cuffs off, hope gone, lights out.

In a cell filled with nothing, I was nothing. Forced to face the ugly reality of nothingness, claustrophobia would be my only companion. There was no one left to listen to my stories and jokes, no one left to confirm my existence. In the free world and even in my prison experience previous to this, I always had a method to deal with my pain and suffering— money and humor. They were distractions from facing the ugly truth of who I really was. I was in Gehenna.

Loneliness took hold. I heard stories about inmates who were so lonely in solitary confinement that they turned on the faucet because it was said that they could hear voices in the running water. As it stood, I heard only screams from beyond my door for what might have been days, weeks, or months. Finally, I climbed out of my bed, made my way to the sink, and turned on the faucet.

Then came the big dark.

A blackness so deep and profound that it could only be realized through auditory assistance. The only glow was a pinhole of dead light still making its way to Earth from a burned-out star in a forgotten galaxy a trillion light years away. There were no more shades of grey. My world lost contrast. My metal bunk became a metal coffin. The sound of the faucet was my new morphine.

Voices emerged from lives, past and present. I heard the moans of my brother Sammy, trapped in the wreckage of his car accident, bleeding and covered in glass. *Help me,* he groaned.

A cold wind swept over me. The temperature plummeted a thousand degrees. I heard my dead brother Jonathan. The remains of a small child sat in the corner crying. *You wasted my life? I died for nothing*, he whispered.

The metal on the bunk above me flexed from its warped shape and improper welds. Fists thudded on the sheet of metal like a gong. Each indent flaked paint chips and rust down over me. My brother Vinny's arm slipped over the edge. His skin was blue. He had overdosed on drugs. *Why didn't you save me,* he hissed.

Acoustic impressions. Only sensory deprivation could allow me to visualize such sounds. The voices continued layering, one upon the other, until they reached a screeching so loud they finally crescendoed with a *snap*.

I opened my eyes and saw shades of white in the darkness. I heard only the sound of the running faucet.

A voice whispered through the water. "Someday, this door will open for you."

"How did you get into my cell?"

Through a tiny trickle of light in the window, I could see a shadow on the far side of my cell near the door. That sliver of light illuminated an exposed forearm wrapped with a koi fish tattoo.

"When the door opens, you will see a path. Do not stray from it."

I swung my feet over the edge of the bed and stepped into liquid. The sink must've overflown in my sleep. There was at least three inches of water on the floor. It was a reddish hue.

How could so much blood come from a single faucet?

I waded through the bloody waters towards the shadow by the door, and with each step closer, the shadow faded into nothingness. I turned on the light to find myself in an empty, dry cell. I looked at the sink. The faucet was still running. I reached over and turned it off.

***

I awakened from my waking nightmare, still in the hole. How long had I been here? One month. Two months. Three months. Four months. Five months. Half a year, nothing. Time was their weapon. Every day I was kept in the SMU was a day of RDAP good time I was losing from the reduction I was promised off of my sentence. The bottom line was that there was bureaucratic paperwork to show the world I had rights. I didn't. I was the prisoner, and they were the guards.

Locked away in the twilight of my six-by-ten cell, I reached out to the Jewish powerhouses in Brooklyn. Rabbi Shmuel Spritzer's legal team contacted the warden at Lewisburg prison on my behalf. The warden stated that he had no idea why I was being held indefinitely without a formal charge. Well past the time limit for a legal investigation, I was ultimately served a fraudulent disciplinary infraction for stealing.

The items that I allegedly stole are issued by FCI prisons to inmates all over the BOP. You can't steal something that is given to you by the prison. In the incident report, no inmate or witness said I sold, bought, or was in possession of any alleged items.

The following week, I was taken upstairs to a holding area and placed in a cage. Two Special Investigative Services officers, who looked like they could have been brother and sister, sat down at the table outside the cell. One was a large lumberjack type of man, and the other an even larger mountain woman.

"I'm Officer Systemic, and this is my partner, Officer Corruption. Tell us about the steroids, drugs, and protein powder at Ray Brook."

"What the fuck does a prison I was at two years ago have to do with now?"

With disdain, Officer Systemic reiterated, "Tell us what you know, and we'll let you go."

"I don't know what you're talking about."

While I may or may not have dabbled in tobacco in Ray Brook, I was never involved with the contraband they wanted information about.

Officer Systemic looked over to Officer Corruption.

"Do we send him to a disciplinary hearing?"

Officer Corruption smirked at me in a sinister manner. I could see the cracks in her glasses. She looked like the actor Michael Douglas in *Falling Down*.

"Take him away."

While there was a list of civil rights violations under the due process clauses of the Fifth and Fourteenth Amendments of the Constitution, I stuck to the facts. One of those rights was the right to face my accusers. My written and verbal requests were both denied before and during my disciplinary hearing.

Throughout my time in prison, I had no disciplinary write-ups, which I thought would have at least afforded me the benefit of the doubt. The Disciplinary Hearing Officer never even opened the report. He placed his hand on top of it as if to verify its existence while stating, "I'm not going to waste anyone's time by calling them as witnesses."

He continued to raise and lower his hand on top of the report. Each time his hand touched upon the report, he repeated himself.

"I'm going to go with the greater weight of the evidence. The greater weight of the evidence. *The greater weight of the evidence.*"

I was found guilty. Anger and frustration boiled inside of me. However, I refused to give them the satisfaction of losing my composure.

"Why was I left in solitary confinement for so long?" My voice was calm.

"To promote respect for the law."

I spent 180 days in solitary confinement. Legally, the punishment for the infraction was thirty days. I guess the other hundred and fifty were on the house.

I had lost all of my potential RDAP good-time credit. Instead of receiving up to a twelve-month reduction in my sentence for completing the RDAP program, I ended up serving an additional thirteen months in prison.

On my last night in the SMU at Lewisburg, I lay in bed awaiting my release... back to prison. That's correct. I was in jail, in prison.

I didn't know I was being maced until I felt the tingling in my throat and eyes. When I tasted the pepper in my mouth, I sealed the vent before the tidal wave of heat filled my lungs. I wrapped a wet shirt around my face and lay on the floor. I felt, at least in that moment, that I had nothing left to desire. I knew that my pain would come to an end.

The cinematic cigarette burns in the top right corner of my brain signaled me to switch reels. A miracle made in a moment of suffering is now a lasting memory of happiness for me. *The Shawshank Redemption* was playing somewhere in the cosmos, and I picked up the radio signal by grace or luck. I was liberated that night in my cell, beyond the four walls surrounding me. To supersede suffering is a powerful sensation, unquantifiable in value. The resilience of the human spirit knows no bounds.

I've met men and women who have spent years in solitary confinement in state and federal prisons across America, and I've read about others who have served decades in the hole. As for me, I was only a guest dropping in for a short visit. For others, it was a lifetime.

As of the writing of this book, Lewisburg Prison has had multiple lawsuits and complaints filed against them. Payments to prisoners have been made to some of those who suffered at the hands of Lewisburg corrections officers. Allegations of abuse and torture at USP Lewisburg have been common and documented throughout history.

28.

After months of transit, I arrived at my final destination. Fort Dix was an old military base that had been converted into a prison. My dad was stationed there during his time in the service. I walked into the same mess hall where I had eaten breakfast with him as a child. The place looked the same, even down to the powdered eggs. As I stood dressed in an orange jumper and Bruce Lee slippers I was struck with nostalgia.

I did my best to shrug it off. I crossed the compound to the transit unit. The inside of the unit was dark and cramped, illuminated only by dim fluorescent bulbs. I saw a man standing across the room from me at the ice machine. I froze, holding my bunk roll across my arms. Disbelief clouded my vision. In an instant, I saw a phantom, a legend, and America's ultimate anti-hero. A man I had admired and spent years of my life trying to become stood in front of me. George Jung.

The same George Jung played by Johnny Depp in the movie *Blow*. The same George Jung I saw posed in photos with DaVinci that hung along the hallway the first day I met him at his condo in downtown Philadelphia. He turned from the ice machine and looked at me briefly before shuffling past me down the hallway.

***

During the remainder of my sentence, I stayed out of trouble. I wanted to get out on time. I followed the rules, and while inmates ate like kings with illegal food from the kitchen, I ate peanut butter and oatmeal. Barbecue, boil, broil, bake, fillet or sauté it. There is no version of peanut butter and oatmeal combined with items from the commissary list humanly possible that I didn't eat. Even the one with racquet balls, I mean none.

The time came and went, but the most iconic moments during my sentence happened when I was alone with only music to hold my hand. I sat wide awake on my bunk during the middle of the night on my last Christmas in prison, eating, you guessed it, peanut butter and oatmeal. Sleep, like my freedom, had been long forgotten years ago. Through the bars on the window, I watched the snow fall to the ground, illuminated by orange exterior lights.

Accumulated tears trickled through Nat King Cole's *The Christmas Song* played in my head. My heart swelled in D flat major. I imagined myself outside these prison walls, beyond the nightmares lit by the buzzing orange lights of Fort Dix. I watched my spirit walk home in the snow as my body stayed put leaving a fresh set of footprints behind.

Jack Frost and Yuletide carols hung in the air. Each nipped at my memories. I hugged my jacket like my long-lost dad to stay warm. From down the street, I could see my childhood illuminated brightly with colorful lights. Each step echoed soft and gentle crunches.

A black door with a gold knocker stood in front of me. Through the window, I could see them at last. Their happiness gave me pause before I pushed my way inside. After years of walking, I was finally home.

As everyone gathered in the living room, I stomped my boots, shook off the snowflakes, and hung my coat like I had a thousand times before. They laughed and smiled as stories from the years were shared. I sat beside my brother as our dog Chestnut warmed himself by the open fire. Love filled the air, and turkey seasoned bright, it was a magical night. My mom sat beside me and hugged me tightly. She was much older now, ninety-two to be exact. Her eyes welled up.

"I missed you, my son. You're so grown up and handsome, but I remember when you were only one. Although it's been said many times, in many ways, I love you."

I awoke from my reverie, alone on that metal bunk, before I could say *I love you* back.

***

His room was near the end of the hall on the left. Other than tending to flowers outside, he seldom left the unit. I saw a mutual friend seated with him through the cell door window. I knocked on the door and was given the okay to enter. We shook hands, he offered me a seat while the other guy stepped out.

Clarity can be loud, but speaking to your role model while sitting in the same prison cell was deafening. I barely remember what I said to the judge who sentenced me, but my conversation with George Jung will be branded in my mind forever.

"Even in the worst circumstances, shaking your hand is an honor," I said.

"Not because of what you did but because you inspired me to roll the dice. I chased your shadow for years. I aspired to be you."

"I appreciate that kid, but you know how many people tell me this," he said in his thick New England accent.

"I know, but those people aren't me. They don't know you, and they damn sure don't know DaVinci."

"DaVinci?" he said, puzzled. "I don't know any DaVinci."

"I saw pictures of the two of you holding whiskey glasses. A Mexican guy from California. He has a koi fish tattoo wrapped around his forearm."

George held his eyes closed, opened them, and stared past me for a moment. I could see the wheels turning as he tried to remember.

"I'm sorry, kid. It's been a long time since I've been involved in that life."

I couldn't believe my ears.

George is wrong. He's old. He doesn't remember.

"The photos, George. You have to remember. I saw the photos with my own eyes. The two of you were standing at a party in someone's yard drinking whiskey."

"Kid, I don't know any DaVinci."

I almost didn't believe him, but then I saw he was serious.

"Are you positive?"

"I'm positive."

My head spun. Almost a decade later, I was no closer to finding DaVinci than when I last saw him in Las Vegas. I felt like a fool for believing that George would have an answer for me. I did my best to conceal my disappointment.

"George, I know you like whiskey and that you're going home soon. So I'd like to help you get a head start on which drink you'll have to celebrate your newfound freedom."

A week prior, I asked my brother Vinny to send me a list of the world's best whiskies. I handed it to George. On the back of the list, I had signed my name and wrote.

Dear George, from one cowboy to another. I hope you get everything you ever wanted in your next life.

"I appreciate the gesture, kid. You'll be fine out there. I know because I've always had a good eye for great things in life."

We shook hands, and whoever I was before that moment was left behind in George's cell that day.

George was nearing the end of his twenty-year prison sentence. What would have become of me had my criminal career continued? The sad reality of isolation and a life lost in time. My admiration for George was outweighed by the sadness that I felt for him. The truth of what had become of him simultaneously broke my heart and granted me deliverance from my love affair with crime.

Fortunately for me, it wasn't the last day of summer, and I always had a door to get back inside... there would be more white horses and pretty ladies at my door.

***

Tonight was my last night in prison. As I lay on my bunk, I reflected on my experiences over the years of incarceration. You either benefit from prison, or you don't. There is no happy medium, hence the seventy percent recidivism rate within five years after release.

Some of the most extraordinary acts of kindness were shown to me by those who had been deemed unforgivable. Men serving life sentences treated me with compassion and taught me that even though we are flawed, we can all learn to love and forgive others. Life is short, and our time on Earth is limited, and there is no time like the present for self-realization.

Whether you're in MDC Brooklyn, Santa Fe Penitentiary, Folsom State, Rikers Island, San Quentin, or USP Florence Colorado, one thing holds true. The most dangerous place to be a prisoner is inside of your own mind.

***

The funeral was at eleven in the morning. I wore my best clothes. Nobody knew that I was the shooter. It was an accident. I didn't mean to do it. It didn't change the way I felt about him. DaVinci was the reason I lived past the age of twenty-five. I loved him like a brother, and I was heartbroken to have to bury my mentor. The casket sat surrounded by white roses in the church. Guests filled the room to maximum occupancy. Flowers were strewn throughout. I signed the registry and went down the list of names to see who had shown up for the viewing. Most of the guests I knew, some I didn't. I fell into the back of the line and waited my turn to pay my respects. Sweat dripped down the inside of my dress shirt. Was it hot because of my suit jacket, or was I nervous? The line shuffled slightly, but I felt like I hadn't moved. I said nothing to the family as I approached the casket, knelt, and prayed.

Arms folded across my chest, I lay in a black suit, staring up at myself. I fell back, startled. I was a guest at my funeral, and it was me in the casket. The family was mine. Panicked, I jumped up and backed away from the casket, shoving people aside as I looked for DaVinci in the crowd. I felt a tugging sensation at my pant legs. Quicksand. Mud-covered hands clawed at me and covered my eyes, ears, and mouth, pulling me into the coffin. I was buried ali ve.

***

The alarm on my watch went off. This was the first and only time I was happy to wake up in prison. I exercised, showered, and one last time, I dressed in khakis. Any form of possible institutionalization that I carried on my back, was pried off, and left behind on my bunk.

The BOP provided me with an outfit to wear home. I'm not saying I was excited walking out of prison dressed in a black turtleneck and jeans, looking like Steve McQueen in the movie *Bullit*, but there would be no more high-speed chases for me. I would've worn a trash bag as long as I got to leave.

I was happy to have finished serving my time and could only hope I was leaving prison a better man than when I entered. I was given an itinerary with a plane ticket and instructed to catch a flight to LAX grab a cab, and go directly to the halfway house.

I was going to Los Angeles to stay with my brother Vinny. While I was incarcerated, he stopped partying, found God, and started a new life with his family away from the crime and poverty of Philadelphia. He was the only stable family member I had left.

The terms of my release were outlined on a bright orange form stating that I was now a convicted felon and may not consort with known felons or possess a firearm. I signed the form and walked out of the building.

I got the message, God! Loud and clear!

My release from Federal prison felt the same as it had when I was released from Glen Mills at age sixteen. Both were a fugacious satisfaction. Time warped and reshaped itself in ways I could never have imagined during my incarceration. I went to eleven different prisons, so in my memory, I only served eleven days. Time was consistently inconsistent. Expansive and nonexistent at once. It felt endless when I was there, but the moments worth remembering were so few and far between that upon reflection, the nine years I had spent inside prison had shrunk into nothingness.

29.

The thrill I felt as we drove across the Ben Franklin Bridge into the heart of Philly was worth the wait. I looked upon it with new eyes and thought about every time I had traversed this bridge in the past on a different walk in life.

To board the plane without proper identification, the BOP provided me with a piece of paper that stated I was fresh out of Federal prison. A boy and his father sat beside me on the plane. This was the first time I had seen or even heard of a digital tablet. I felt like a monkey who had been shot into outer space. There was no such thing as an iPad before I went to prison, and by the time I was being released, so was the iPhone 6.

As I scratched my head in confusion, he noticed my perplexed look. The boy was polite and friendly.

"Hi, my dad and I are going on a vacation. He lets me play my favorite apps on Wi-Fi if I use Bluetooth."

Not knowing what the fuck he just said, I thought to myself, wow, how far the world has come that this kid speaks German at such a young age.

Impressive.

The engines began to whirl as we lined up on the runway. I didn't look back as the plane taxied down the tarmac. Philly gave me an unstoppable heart to overcome life. For that, I'll always be grateful and love you forever. My eyes faded shut.

***

I sized up the pros and cons when checking into the halfway house. The pros were career criminals, and the cons were, well, were exactly that, convicts. It was the same shitty bunk, the same shitty mattress, and the same shitty people, but the difference was that I had partial access to the free world, which gave me some sense of normality.

While most people didn't have a job interview, my brother Vinny did the heavy lifting to help fix my life and set me up with a job within one week of my arrival in Los Angeles. After years of working for pennies per hour in Federal prison, I was willing to do whatever it would take to get back on my feet. I was determined to contribute to the world in a positive way. I wanted to prove my worth to my family, friends, and, most importantly, myself. Pride took a back seat.

Ninety days later, I was cleared to go home early on house arrest. I packed up my property, walked outside, and went to catch the bus.

An hour later, I showed up at Vinny's house unannounced. I put my bags down, slapped my face, scrambled my hair, and started breathing heavily as I banged on the door. When he opened the door, he froze in shock. I stared at him in panic.

"I couldn't do it. It's too much. I didn't know what to do, so I took off.

Can I hide out here for a few days?"

He was paralyzed, speechless.

"Relax, I'm fucking with you!" I yelled.

I hugged him tight and lifted him off the ground to make sure he remembered that hug for the rest of his life.

***

On my first night at home, I had dinner with my brother and his family to celebrate my release. I looked across the table at my brother and then around at his family. He had a wife and two beautiful daughters.

"It's a miracle that we both made it out of that city alive," I said.

"It's not a miracle. It's God's plan," he said.

"Jesus Christ," I said.

"Exactly," he said.

"Don't start, Vinny."

After dinner, I took a hot shower and looked in a real mirror for the first time since before I was sent to prison. The only mirror in prison was an eleven by seventeen highly polished piece of stainless steel, which only provided a murky, distant reflection. In some strange way, seeing myself in that mirror was confirmation that I still existed, if only in part.

That night, while I lay in a fresh, clean bed for the first time in years, I calculated the exact number of days I served in prison. I assumed it was around two thousand, but no more than that. Perhaps I didn't want to know the total cost and just wanted to pay my bill. In total, I spent 2922 days in the custody of the Bureau Of Prisons.

After three months of house arrest, I would start a five-year term of probation. I hoped to be granted early termination for good behavior. I still had a long journey ahead of me.

***

Almost fifteen years had passed since I met DaVinci for the first time. After that first meeting, my brother Vinny told me that DaVinci would usher us into the Golden Age of drug dealing. Stepping back into the free world, I realized that maybe he was correct. I had no desire to break the law when I was released from prison, but I couldn't help but notice how limited those types of opportunities had become in the modern world. I once moved in and out of the corridors of crime without detection, but technology had evolved so rapidly that the days of fake passports, stolen cars, and carefree drug trafficking had come to an end.

During my incarceration, I spent countless days dreaming of the beautiful things I missed from the free world. When I was first arrested, I missed the simple things like my clothes, cars, and homes. Once I adjusted to wearing a khaki uniform and living in a cell, I began to miss the more important things like my family, high- quality food, and privacy.

Eventually, I came to miss the most basic human interactions. These interactions were something I had never noticed or appreciated when I was free. I'm referring to a simple hello from a neighbor or a nod from a stranger passing on the street. I'd realized that these little acts of civility were the cornerstones of life. They were confirmation that I was a human being and that I existed in the real world. It frightened me to think of how much my self-worth depended on those minor interactions. I thought back to the first time I met Lana. She pulled up next to me at a red light and waved. Now, when I pull up to a red light, all I see are people looking down at their phones.

If a man walks down the street and no one looks up to acknowledge him, does he exist?

On my first trip back to Philly after my release from prison, I decided to walk around the city and get a feel for the world I remembered so well before my decade-long, involuntary vacation. It felt good to be back on the sidewalk. The smell of concrete and asbestos was invigorating. I took my time, soaking in the texture and vibrations of the city. The streets were buzzing.

I took a stroll down Allegheny Avenue and saw a homeless black man sitting on the sidewalk, head down, holding a cardboard sign that read *Made in America*.

"At least we still make something in this country," I mustered disgracefully, mimicking a relic of some rust belt, blue-collar cliche I'd heard over the years from embittered men— most of whom had lost their manufacturing jobs decades ago. I couldn't judge any of these people because, after all, I was one of them, but it was brutal to see such truth in suffering outside of a prison. A cold reminder that I was also made in America. We all were. And therein lies the dilemma. An identity that feels impossible to look in the eyes without remorse.

A mad preacher called out to me from across the street. His eyes were fiery, and he clutched a red book, the front of which was inscribed with a language I couldn't recognize.

"You!" he said. "You still have a chance! Save yourself! Because no one is coming to save you."

I continued down Allegheny, and as I rounded the corner onto Kensington Avenue, I heard gunfire somewhere in the distance. A domestic dispute or another school shooting, I'm sure. Maybe gang violence... I suppose they're all domestic disputes. Doesn't really matter. Shootings are shootings, and there are more than enough to go around.

I hope I never get shot. I've been close many times, but all I have is gunpowder and deafening silence to show for it. I know many people that have been shot. Some survived, some didn't. I suppose I'm one of the lucky ones. I wonder what they would write on my gravestone if I were finally shot to death and given a proper burial.

"He lived the whole crisis. They found the shell casings nearby. Death came for him Americanly."

Not bravely, not heroically, but *Americanly*. Those would be fair enough words, I suppose. All is fair if a man dies on his nation's own soil without the undignified restraint of shackles and handcuffs. What else can a man ask for in a legacy?

I continued down Kensington Avenue, and as I walked, I saw two sides of a single world, a world desperately in need of a collective revolution of thought. A world divided unforgivingly by a blazing hot set of train tracks. On one side of the tracks, electric luxury cars lined the street in front of modern glass condos. People wandered by, lost in an endless flickering scroll of hyperbolic reproductions of the natural world. On the other side of the tracks, zombies lurked in the shadows, frozen in drug-induced stress positions, backlit by trash barrel fires, illuminating the faces of broken-hearted spirits who had long ago given up on the American dream.

In the middle of those blazing hot tracks stood a leather-clad apparition, the shape of the uncanny valley, unleashing a hail of automatic gunfire into the Philadelphia night. It was tech-noir realized, and John Connor was nowhere to be found.

I could still hear the mad preacher calling out behind me in the distance.

"Save yourself. The way is still open."

While I may have been living under a rock for the past decade, the truth of that rock is, that it sheltered me from the nuclear fallout of a mass tech revolution, which groomed and domesticated people in this brave new world to detach themselves from the life cycle, while forfeiting their privacy, identity, and personal freedoms.

Vinny was correct about the Golden Age, but I failed to realize that it wasn't just the Golden Age of drug dealing. It was the Golden Age of America and the prime of our lives. The world I remembered before I went to prison would live only in my heart and mind. There would be no Renaissance. The Golden Age had come to an end.

WINTER

30.

On my first vacation after my release, I had a layover at Harry Reid International Airport on my way to Denver. I noticed a woman who was shivering from the cold air conditioning in the airport.

I offered her my jacket that lay across the top of my suitcase. She initially declined, but I insisted, and she gratefully accepted. I got up to let her take my seat as we waited for the inter-connecting flight.

As she warmed up to me, we sat down next to each other and began chatting about where she was from, her life, her kids, and her family. She had recently retired from working with the government, and to celebrate her retirement, she was flying to Colorado to visit the Rocky Mountain National Park.

"Which department?" I asked.

"I worked in the BOP," she said.

"Oh, I'm familiar with the BOP, Code of Federal Regulations, and the United States Legal Code," I said.

"I assume you also work in government. Are you a lawyer or something?" she laughed.

Because she was a stranger at the airport rather than a next-door neighbor, I decided to be honest with her and share a little bit about my life.

"Lawyer, no, but... ah... yes, I was with the Feds."

Excited that she was right, she exclaimed, "I knew it. Which department, the DEA, FBI?"

Realizing that she misunderstood my statement, I leaned over, touched the chair between us, smiled, and said, "No. I was *with* the Feds."

There was an immediate paradigm shift once she realized what I meant. Her facial expression dialed out. She became nervous, panicked, and desperately sought a way to escape our conversation.

"Oh, I'm sorry, my phone is ringing, and I need to take it," she said.

I looked at her perplexed. "It's on the charger. And it's dead."

"I, I think my mom is calling me," she stuttered.

Confused again, I replied, "But from what you told me, she's dead too."

She thanked me for the jacket, set it on the chair, and took off.

One minute, I was the nicest guy in the world, and the next, I was damaged. From day one in prison, I was constantly reminded that I was a felon and would be treated accordingly.

I watched the term *felon* consume the identity of other inmates. They would wear that identity to the point where they forgot they could be something else. The truth is that seventy percent of the prison population consists of nonviolent first- time drug offenders, and being one of them, I wasn't exempt from such a stigma. I accepted that my actions had consequences, and some of those consequences would have long-standing effects on my life.

31.

Three years later...

When we spoke of each other, we shared one thing in common. She told me that I saved her life, and I told her that she had saved mine.

"I trust you with my life," Selene said.

This is the most prestigious compliment that a person can pay you. The last person other than Selene to say this to me was DaVinci. The first time I saw her, I knew that she was special. She was a client at the business where I worked, and even though I had worked there for years, we had only met once. She came in on a Saturday that I was covering for the boss. I noticed Selene struggling to tie her shoe due to severe pain in her back and offered to help. The following day, she called the store to speak with me.

"I just wanted to say thank you. As it was nice for an absolute stranger to go completely out of their way to be a gentleman and do something kind without any expectations of something in return."

Within a month, we were inseparable.

Selene was South African, had strawberry blonde hair, and was the living definition of what I pictured in my heart as my wife. We came from two completely different walks of life. Selene had followed all of the rules. She was a billionaire from Malibu Beach who came from an elite class of society. She had everything that she needed. She owned multiple homes, two jets, and a fleet of luxury cars.

I was a convicted felon from Philadelphia who came from a broken home. I had shattered every rule in existence. I had no house, no car, no money. I had nothing to offer her except for myself, along with my freedom from desire for material things. We were the unlikeliest pair.

However, we each carried our own peculiar life predicament. Selene revealed to me that, despite the appearance of a perfect marriage, she and her husband, Dr. Julius Non, were effectively living in an unofficial divorce. We spoke often about the complexities of her life and marital woes. She felt betrayed, heartbroken, and abandoned. To ensure the truth of their marriage would be known, she kept a journal for the last thirteen years, intending for it to be discovered after her passing. Hearing this elegant woman share such a terrible pain broke my heart.

I found myself in an emotionally compromising situation. Selene cared deeply for me and simply loved to love. She was older, classy, and generous with her affection. Still, I couldn't help but wonder — why me, why was I so lucky? So I did my best to support her, becoming what she needed most but never had: someone to listen.

Selene said she had begged her husband for a divorce, but he refused and warned her not to open Pandora's box. She stated his refusal was mainly for financial reasons. I was concerned for her welfare, knowing it would be hard to protect her if I was still on probation. She wanted out, and I understood why. Selene wasn't free. Neither was I.

***

It was Valentine's Day and dinner was at eight. Selene set a reservation for us and two other couples at Providence, a Five Star Diamond Award recipient from The American Academy of Hospitality Sciences. Selene chose to dine there to ensure that our night was perfect. I wore black slacks and a white dress shirt. She wore a greenish blue, single-shoulder dress with earrings to match. She looked stunning.

I joked when the other couples walked in, "I'd like to introduce you to my wife."

We all laughed, but little did they know the struggle Selene and I were going through to free her from her unhappiness.

We sat at the best table in the house, dead center and upfront near the band. I sat on Selene's left as we dined and laughed our way into the night. While others were celebrating, we were planning our future together.

"I spoke with an advisor. I'm going to leave him, and I want to marry you," she said.

"If all goes well, I should be off probation by this time next year. It's important to me that I take your hand under God as a free man."

Our plan was for her to divorce Julius and for me to terminate my probation early. We would get married on the beach, just the two of us. To help ensure this all went seamlessly, Selene drafted a letter to the U.S. Federal Probation Office. I could hardly contain my excitement about our freedom and future together. A week from now we would be celebrating her birthday, and a year from her birthday we would be getting married. It was an incredible night, and the world was at our fingertips.

***

It was July in the summer of 2018. Selene was on holiday in France with her husband, but we were desperate to see each other, so she devised a way to come back home to visit me. She told her family that she needed to return to California for a check-up with her spinal surgeon.

She landed at John Wayne Airport in Orange County. When she came out to the arrival area, I hugged her, handed her five dozen roses, grabbed her bags, and pointed to the car.

"Right this way. How was the flight?" I asked.

"It was good. Funny enough I saw a business associate of my husband's on the plane."

I laughed. "Did you tell him I said hello?"

After a long flight, all she wanted to do was relax. We usually split time between my place and hers depending on our need for privacy. With her home being empty, it was just the two of us. We had dinner and retired to bed sometime around midnight.

As we lay down I pretended to drop the remote, reached under the bed, and pulled out a gift I had prepared for her. It was a painting we had found while shopping together a year earlier. I returned later to buy the painting, but it had been sold. I spent months tracking it down.

"It's the painting you loved. I found it," I said.

"How? It was a year ago that we saw this... I can't believe you found it. I love it! I have an idea. Let's hang it up in our new home."

I kissed her goodnight and wrapped my arm around her. Selene fell asleep on my chest with my hand intertwined with hers. For once, my life made sense. As I fell asleep, I thought of what a lovely thing it was that she had said to me about our future home. It would be a beautiful memory to look forward to.

***

Before Selene returned to France for the remainder of the summer, Selene and I went to look at the wedding rings she had picked out for us. We both chose one, but mine needed resizing, so I'd return to get it fitted at the end of the week when she flew back to France. The letter Selene wrote on my behalf to help me get off probation was sent to my lawyer. He petitioned the courts for an early termination of my probation.

I held her hand the entire way back to the airport. I began to miss her before she was even gone. My birthday was the following week. Knowing that I missed many birthdays in prison, Selene asked me repeatedly what I wanted. Adamantly I told her, "I only want you."

Over the next week, I stayed at Selene's house to take care of her maid, Alice, who was sixty-eight years old and undergoing chemotherapy and radiation treatment for cancer. Selene had hired me to take care of Alice who had become sick over the last few months. Alice lived alone in the guest house and needed someone on call. Selene was worried about her health and felt that I was the only person she trusted enough to care for Alice.

Selene and I kept in touch throughout the remainder of her vacation in France. We reminded each other to keep calling the probation office for a status update about my potential early termination. My lawyer felt I had a legitimate shot at having it granted due to my exceptional record.

Three weeks before Selene was scheduled to return from France, I received a phone call from Alice. The voicemail she left was frantic and inaudible. There was some kind of emergency at Selene's house.

I ripped through the streets at over a hundred miles an hour. On average, it was a twenty-four-minute drive from my house to Selene's house. I made it there in sixteen minutes flat.

I punched in the code to open the garage, and by the time it started to open, I was already bent down, crawling underneath the door. I paused, confused. Selene's car was gone.

"They robbed the bedroom!" Alice cried out when I rushed into the home.

A police officer walked into the kitchen.

"Who are you, and what are you doing here? This is an active crime scene."

While I slept that morning, I had several missed calls and text messages from Selene asking me to go to her house. She was concerned that something had happened to Alice. Selene's entire family was in France, so she asked me to go over and check on her. She was obviously concerned, and so was I, given Alice's state of health.

I FaceTimed Selene and gave the police officer my phone so they could see what had happened in the home. I stood at the end of the hall and listened to the police officer explain to Selene and her husband that two safes had been stolen from the closet in the primary bedroom. The officer came back to the kitchen and handed me my phone.

The rest of the home was untouched. Julius and Selene's computers were still there, including Selene's shoe collection and numerous other valuables that were left behind.

No one knew my legal name. No one knew I was a felon. No one knew I lived here with her. No one knew we loved each other. No one knew Selene was my fiancé. I had no idea what'd fully happened, but I knew the immediate repercussions of a situation like this would cause severe damage to both of us.

Once the officer returned my phone, I called Selene back. The cops were yelling at me to stop moving throughout the home, but I was doing my best to help Selene understand what was happening while trying not to get arrested. Ignoring them, I stepped outside to speak with her.

"Selene, this isn't going to end well for me."

She didn't have much to say, neither did I. We both knew I was right.

"I'll call you back when I have an update," I said.

When I reentered the house, a female officer approached me and began a relentless line of questioning. When she ran my social security number, I knew that I would show up in the NCIC as a felon. She asked me to step into the garage with her, along with another officer.

"We ran your name. You lied," she said.

It was true, and I had given a different name. I hadn't gone by my legal birth name since I was a kid. This isn't something that I would typically try to conceal. The name I'd given the police was the name that even my probation officer addressed me by. The police stated that I might be cited for interfering with an active investigation. I knew that the mitigating circumstances would be enough to help me explain my improper identification, but as for the rest of it, I wasn't so sure. One week before the robbery, Selene and I were at her home together on camera. Her supposed visit home to see her spinal doctor had been well documented on the home surveillance system. There would be no explanation for that other than the truth.

So here I was, in the middle of a crime scene investigation, trying not to be arrested, stay out of jail, not violate my probation, and simultaneously protect Selene. My life was in the air, and I had no idea where it would land.

The police officer approached me and told me not to leave the property. I stepped back outside and called Selene.

"Are you all right?" she asked.

"No, Selene, I'm not."

Her voice breaking.

"I need you to be strong. Be strong for both of us."

"I will. You have my word. I woke up today, I thought Alice was dying, I ran into the fire, and I did it for you."

I could hear her trembling on the other end of the phone.

"I know."

The line was silent. We both listened. The silence was the sound of us being torn apart. I spoke.

"They are going to try and arrest me. I have to go." Dying on the inside, I said, "Goodbye, my love."

A police officer crept along the driveway toward me. In my peripheral, I felt him coming closer. He jumped on me, grabbed my arm, and pulled it behind my back.

"I need you to put these on."

I was handcuffed and shoved into the back of a police car and told to sit tight.

"The detective's on his way."

I was twenty-one the last time I had a million dollars in front of me. Give me that same million dollars today, and I'd bet it all that I'd never be in handcuffs again for the rest of my life. I would have lost that bet. Here I was, back in handcuffs, but I hadn't committed a crime, nor had I violated any of DaVinci's seven rules.

The back door of the police car opened, and light poured in. The detective stepped in front of the sun, blocking it out with his silhouette. I was the prime suspect, and this large, bald, Italian detective had only one thing to say to me.

"Tell us you did it."

I stared at him with a blank expression. I felt nothing. I lived here with my soon- to-be wife. This wasn't happening.

"Confess, just confess, man. We'll get you a deal. Come on, you know how this works," the detective said.

Over and over, the detective insisted I did it. I was told they would work with me and give me a deal, but I would have to confess now.

"Tell you what? I'm innocent!" I yelled.

"Hang tight," the detective said and closed the car door.

Hang tight? Where the fuck was I going? I'm locked in the back of a police car. The detective opened the door to ask me more questions. I stopped him and said, "I have a question for you."

"What's that?" he replied.

"I need to know, am I going to prison tonight, or will I be waking up in my own bed? My birthday is tomorrow, and mentally— I have to prepare for that."

"We're still debating whether or not you robbed the house."

I got the fucking message, God! Loud and fucking clear!

After a few hours, I was taken out of the car, escorted to the outside patio, seated at a table, and bombarded with questions.

"Do you know anyone who would want to rob the home? Where were you last night? Are you willing to give up the GPS records on your phone? Do the husband and wife argue? How does the wife look? Do you need a lawyer? Are you nervous? You seem nervous. Anything suspicious about the robbery?"

"I have absolutely nothing to do with this," I told them.

"You're the only one other than the maid who had access to the house."

"You guys need to check my resume. I was a hustler, not a two-bit junkie robbing houses."

"Oh, we have, and as thin as your profile is, it's quite heavy. That's why he's here."

The detective nodded his head, referencing the DEA agent at the table. After an hour-long interrogation, they placed me back inside the police car.

I was eventually released a few hours later and instructed not to leave town. The police listed me as a suspect and told me they would contact me if they needed anything further.

Days passed. I hadn't slept and had no idea what was happening or how to reach Selene without getting in trouble. Every law enforcement agency was looking at me under a microscope. Only in recent times had I been able to scrape together a small savings of twenty-five thousand. I worked legal side jobs to make cash, which I entrusted to Selene. She kept it safe, in the now missing safe. She was the only person who knew everything about me. She was the beneficiary of my bank account, and I trusted her with my life.

I waited.

Since my release from prison, I hadn't had any issues, but now I was looking at multiple probation violations and being charged for falsely identifying myself during a police investigation. Not to mention, I was the prime suspect in a 1.5 million dollar robbery of my girlfriend's home and looking at twenty-five years in prison if wrongfully convicted.

I never said a word.

My loyalty was with her no matter what. I chose to protect her and our relationship, even at the potential cost of my freedom. I wasn't bothered about losing my money or being accused of a crime that I didn't commit. What bothered me most was losing Selene. The moment I lost her, I was back in prison, isolated from love. Despite all of my efforts to contact her both directly and indirectly, I never spoke to Selene again. There is no happy ending to this part of my life.

The guys who robbed her home were arrested less than two months after the incident. I saw the news report on TV. Still, she never reached out. Even after their confessions, her husband was adamant that I was involved and contacted the detective to have me questioned. Once again, I cooperated and was fully exonerated from any connection to the crime.

"I'm sorry about what happened to you that day," the detective said.

"I forgive you. I understand that you're just doing your job. Please just make sure that Selene knows the truth."

Even though Selene's husband used the police as an instrument to harass me, I never said a word. Soon after, I received a call from the U.S. probation office.

"Hello?" I said.

"This is the United States Probation Department. I'd like to speak with you for a moment."

"What can I do for you?"

"I need you to answer one question."

I expected the same question the detective asked earlier. Something like: *tell us you did it.* Instead, it was: "Did Selene know you were a felon when you worked at the house taking care of the maid who was ill?

"Yes."

"Can you prove it?"

Why he asked this specific question is that when on Federal probation you must disclose to any employer that you are a felon.

"Yes, I can prove it."

Thanks to the second sentence in Selene's letter, I could.

He was very honest with me and just after I met him he told me about his past and the situation he was in with regards to being on probation following his incarceration.

The only reason I did not go to prison in regards to his question was because of the second sentence in Selene's letter.

The United States District Judge, Assistant U.S. Attorney, and the U.S. Probation Office on February 26th, 2019, five days after when we were supposed to get married, granted me early termination of my probation.

People have asked me if doing time in prison was hard. The gift and curse about not feeling time anymore is that I now live unconditionally in the moment. So, if I say I love you, no matter how long it's been from when I first said it. I'll be right there, waiting for you, living in the moment.

The total time it took me to earn my freedom was 4191 days, but I always say, it was nothing in comparison to losing love.

32.

I remember only a few before and after moments in my life. The significant ones are the days when my heart was snatched from my hands. You don't know how far you are willing to go until you're already there. I wanted an explanation, but each time I spoke of my life with someone in the hopes of finding an answer, it only exhausted me more.

Hours, weeks, and months melted away as I sat in constant thought, removed from the world, trying to understand what had happened. Lost, tired, and broken, I sought refuge in the two remaining people that I truly trusted: my brothers.

Sammy felt bad about what had happened but encouraged me to be happy. He had known his own lost love. Years after his car accident, the woman he was going to marry was in a severe car accident as well and died. For years, she visited him in the hospital, but in the end, it was him visiting her to say goodbye.

"I wasn't happy, I chose to get high and I fucked up. Follow God. Trust in him unconditionally. He's the author of that which we don't understand, but he'll never fail you, little bro. How do I know? Because I'm still here, ain't I."

How could I feel bad for myself? Not once in his entire life had my brother ever complained about his personal circumstances. I found love in this, I found humility, and I found hope.

Vinny pulled no punches. He didn't deny that I loved Selene, but he knew that my hesitation prevented me from believing that I was worthy of being loved. He said that a house built on a rocky foundation always had a chance that it would collapse. There can be no surprise when you know the risk involved. I knew he was right and hated myself for failing to see the truth sooner.

"I don't have all the answers, but I was right there in Philly with you. Fuck yeah, I was afraid to change, and I had no idea how to do it, but I did. Yes, we had a rough life, but you have to take responsibility for your actions," Vinny said.

"How?" I asked.

"I surrendered. I accepted the things that I couldn't change and rebuilt myself one day at a time. My family depended on me, and I knew the only one who would stop me, was me," Vinny said.

Both of my brothers were brave enough to take on their own demons. I suppose it was time for me to take on mine.

DaVinci taught me that water is the source of life. I wrote down the names of everyone that I felt had betrayed me over the course of my life. After days of self- reflection, I gathered my pages, bought a bottle with a cork, and headed for the beach.

Sand, as far as I could see, every grain represented the multitude of lives I could have lived.

Where am I? I know where I am, but where am I exactly?

I stood staring into the bright center of life. With each crashing wave, my feet sank deeper into the sand. I held the bottle by its neck, ready to cast it into the waves. A part of me wanted to drift out to sea and follow it wherever it may go.

Overwhelmed with emotion, visions came in waves.

Selene's hand pulled me down the beach. Unable to see her face, I felt her warm, vibrant smile as it touched my skin. I tasted her scent on my lips mixed with the salt of the ocean. I kissed her to tell her how I felt. As daylight faded, we walked across the line of the sunset and disappeared in time.

"To know life is to know suffering. To know love is to know loss. When you close your eyes, you will see me... remember me under the sun," Selene said.

Her hand slid out from mine. The waves of love retreated across my mind. I closed my eyes as clouds poured in and burned away the dying light. A love lost in the dark, I tried to make it right.

Floating on my bunk, I awoke in my cell, soaked in a desert of loneliness. A concrete beach lay beneath my feet. She was gone, but my socks were still wet with grains of sand. I stood up and looked out the window at the beach. My hand touched the wall. It collapsed like a sandcastle. The near and distant memories of my life curled, arched, and then broke on the shore. I faded into the nothingness.

The waves washed out. My right hand hung at my side. A small hand's fingertips slipped into mine. I stood with my daughter. She looked up at me. Her beautiful face radiated love.

"Hi, Daddy," she said.

All at once, I smiled, laughed, and cried.

"I'm sorry I never met you," I said through tears.

"It's okay, I know you love me, you gave me these."

She looked up at me to display the most beautiful aqua-green eyes I'd ever seen. My heart kissed her soul. Butterflies formed a veil around her dirty blonde hair. The faculties of my love could not compare to her gentleness. She was my kindred flame. My light that had always shined in the dark. A moment with her was a miracle in time.

"I've got nothing left," I said.

The waves washed out. I looked down. My feet were buried in the sand over my ankles. The waves washed in. Intrinsically connected, Lana now stood beside me, holding my hand.

"I'm angry, Lana."

"Angry at who?"

"The world, everyone," I trembled.

"Why? They didn't do this to you. You know the truth. It's been inside of you the entire time. You just keep denying it," she said.

She pulled my hand to her cheek and kissed the inside of it. I closed my eyes.

I knew she was right. We listened to the swash of the waves. I squeezed her hand tight.

"Hold onto me," I said.

Love of the highest caliber is a love that's free. Knowing she will leave doesn't deter me. Time waits for no one. If I had to go through it all again, knowing what I know now, I would do it the exact same way.

"What are you holding onto?" Sammy asked.

I opened my eyes. My brother stood next to me. He was as healthy and handsome as ever. Lana was gone. My hand was filled with wet sand.

"The past, I suppose. A ghost of myself," I replied.

"Let go, man. Just let go," Sammy said.

"I can't."

"You can. Look at me. I let go. No more wheelchair, no more suffering. I am who I've always been. Myself."

"I don't want this anymore," I said.

"You think I wanted this? Twenty years in a wheelchair? You have no excuse. Stop blaming the world for your mistakes. You know who's responsible. That's who goes in the bottle."

Sammy shook my hand and hugged me.

"You know what you have to do," he said as he walked away down the beach.

I stared out into the waves crashing across the sands of time. My sun had finally set. The answer had always been right in front of me. The bottle was in my left hand, and the pages were in my right. I let go.

The pages flew off into the air.

I pried the cork off, placed the bottle near my mouth, whispered only my name inside, and resealed it. I threw the bottle into the ocean. It was the one thing I needed to do but had never done. I forgave myself, for I had betrayed myself, because I always had a choice.

FIN

SPRING

Epilogue

Time passed, and life went on. I left California and moved into a townhome in Delray Beach, Flordia and took a job selling drugs for a pharmaceutical company, ironically. I spent my free time writing and enjoyed the freedom of riding my motorcycle on the open roads. Occasionally, I still mentored people in physical fitness with their form, breathing, and technique.

I was on my way home from the gym one day, and as I pulled into the driveway, I noticed a parcel envelope leaning against the front door of my townhome. I picked up the envelope, brought it inside, and opened it.

A single embossed piece of stationery was tri-folded inside. At the top of the letter was a logo. Two koi fish overlapped each other to form an infinity symbol. Is this some fancy Chinese buffet?

My heart raced. Anxiety rushed through my body. My hand began to shake. There was a single sentence written in bold letters on the top of the paper beneath the infinity symbol.

Rule number 8: *Always have a backup plan.*

I stared at the letter in disbelief. My eyes crept down the page. There were three points inside of a square that formed a triangle. Next to the point on the left were the words, *water is the source of life*. I turned the paper over and looked at the backside. It was blank. I looked inside the envelope again. A single key sat at the bottom.

***

Two days later, my flight touched down at Philadelphia International Airport. I left town without telling anyone, and no one in my family knew I was coming home. Over the prior two days, my thoughts had swirled wildly. I wasn't sure if I was excited, terrified, or having a mental breakdown.

I rented a car at the airport and drove directly to a hardware store. From there, I drove away from Philadelphia into the countryside. I knew exactly where to go.

As I drove, the words played over and over in my head.

Water is the source of life. You can always find your peace in the waterfall.

I pulled into the same parking lot I had pulled into almost twenty years ago. Paranoid, I looked around before opening the trunk to retrieve a daypack and a shovel. I kept telling myself that the Feds were watching. This was a trap. Fuck it. I need to know. Before I reached the trailhead, I stopped and listened hard... nothing but the sound of the summer breeze moving through the trees.

An eery sensation crept through my body as I made my way up the trail. Déjà vu. I felt like I was retracing steps from a past life rather than a past experience.

I spent years in prison trying to solve the mystery of his disappearance and spent the subsequent years convincing myself that he didn't exist. Time had muddied the waters of objective reality. Nonetheless, I held on to a glimmer of hope.

I arrived at the lagoon and found the hidden trail that led me to the top of the waterfall. I triangulated the position between the waterfall and two adjacent trees. The arcs led me to a meeting point where my backup plan would have been buried. It was approximately twenty-one paces from where we had our conversation.

The sun broke through the trees and splashed on my back. Sweat poured down my face. The mud was thick. I struggled to hack through roots with the shovel. I stopped periodically to pop my head up from the hole, look around, and ensure no one was coming. I dug through the morning into the afternoon. Nothing. I climbed out of the hole, covered in filth.

I argued with myself in the woods while I paced around the hole.

It's a pipe dream. Someone is fucking with you.

I dropped the shovel and walked to the waterfall. I peered down into the swirling pool beneath me. Rocks jutted out from the edges of the lagoon. I felt a rumbling deep inside.

Even if I only broke my legs, I'd never be able to crawl out of here. No one will ever find me.

I thought back to the first phone call that I made to Sammy after my sentencing. The first day that I valued my life.

It was a long way down but twice as long swimming up.

I picked up the shovel and dug deeper.

I'm a gravedigger, toiling in the soil, resurrecting the dead.

The tip of the shovel struck a rock. I leveraged my foot on the edge of the shovel to pry it up and out of the way. It wouldn't budge. I reached in with my hands and cleared a lip in the dirt around the rock. It was no rock, but a boulder. I grabbed onto the lip edge and pulled with all my might. It took every ounce of strength. I yelled in rage. The boulder came loose. I fell back on my ass, covered in mud. A piece of plastic stuck out of the dirt. I wiped away the dirt to reveal a metal briefcase within.

DaVinci kept his word.

Exhausted, physically and mentally, I struggled to catch my breath. Tears streamed from my eyes. I picked myself up and hoisted the briefcase out of the hole. I carried the briefcase to a nearby log and sat down to rest. Minutes passed, and I finally caught my breath. I stared at the briefcase, and when my heart rate subsided, I heard only the sounds of nature.

The rush of the waterfall took center stage. From it arose a cacophony of voices, much like the ones I heard from the running faucet in solitary confinement. These ones, however, spoke to me with grace. Among the discordance, a single voice emerged.

"I just came to say goodbye."

I jumped up from the log and spun around in circles. I looked long and hard in every direction. Nothing. There was no one else there. I was, as I always have been and always will be... alone. I finally stepped out of the mist. I was the only fallen tree in the forest, and I was at peace.

Notes

Chapter 1

1. Boingo, Oingo. "Dead Man's Party." Dead Man's Party. 1985

2. *Journey to the Center of the Earth. Directed by Henry Levin, Cooga Mooga Film Productions, Inc., Joseph M. Schenck Enterprises, Inc., 1959.*

3. Lee, Stan and Ditko, Steve. The Amazing Spider-Man.

Chapter 2

1. Assumption BVM Church. Feasterville-Trevose, PA.

Chapter 3

1. Hill, Patty and Hill, Mildred J. "Happy Birthday." 1893.

Chapter 5

1. Edison Detention Center. Doylestown, PA.

Chapter 7

>1. *Law and Order.* NBC. New York, NY.

Chapter 8

>1. *The Truman Show.* Directed by Peter Weir, Scott Rudin Productions, 1998.

>2. The Glen Mills Schools. Glenn Mills, PA.

Chapter 9

>1. Eagles. "Hotel California." Hotel California. 1977

Chapter 12

>1. Jung, George. 2021.

>2. *Blow.* Directed by Ted Demme, Spanky Pictures, Aposte, 2001.

>3. *Die Hard.* Directed by John McTiernan, Gordon Company and Silver Pictures, 1988.

Chapter 14

>1. Camarena-Salazar, Enrique. "Kiki." 1985.

>2. Caesars Atlantic City. Atlantic City, NJ.

>3. *Die Hard.* Directed by John McTiernan, Gordon Company and Silver Pictures, 1988.

Chapter 15

1. McCartney, Paul. "Maybe I'm Amazed." McCartney. 1970.

Chapter 18

1. Philadelphia Police 15th District. Philadelphia, PA.

2. "Sesame Street." PBS, 1969-2007.

Chapter 20

1. Wynn Las Vegas. Las Vegas, NV.

Chapter 22

1. "The Price is Right." CBS, 1972-2007.

2. Birdland. Kyoto, Japan.

Chapter 23

1. FCI Ray Brook. Raybrook, NY.

2. Justice Prisoner and Alien Transportation System "ConAir". The U.S. Marshals' Justice.

3. Bureau of Prisons (BOP). Washington, D.C.

4. U.S. Immigration and Customs Enforcement (ICE). Washington, D.C.

5. Oklahoma Federal Transfer Center. Oklahoma City, OK.

6. *Escape from Alcatraz.* Directed by Don Siegel, The Malpaso Company, 1979.

7. *Rumble Fish.* Directed by Francis Ford Coppola, Zoetrope Studios, 1983.

8. *Body Heat.* Directed by Lawrence Kasdan, The Ladd Company, 1981.

Chapter 25

1. *Groundhog Day.* Directed by Harold Ramis, Trevor Albert and Harold Ramis, 1993.

2. Holmesburg Prison. Philadelphia, PA

3. Curran-Fromhold Correctional Facility. Philadelphia, PA.

Chapter 27

1. FCI Canaan. Waymart, PA.

2. The Residential Drug Abuse Program (RDAP).

3. Lee, Bruce. "The Way of the Intercepting Fist." 1971.

4. *Falling Down.* Directed by Joel Schumacher, Le Studio Canal + Regency Enterprises, Alcor Films, 1993.

5. Pat the Bat: *USA v. Cody et al, 09-m-185 EDNY, (2009)*

6. United States Penitentiary, Lewisburg. Lewisburg, PA.

7. Spritzer, Rabbi Shmuel. Brooklyn, NY. https://www.jewishprisoner.com

8. *The Shawshank Redemption.* Directed by Frank Darabont, Castle

Rock Entertainment, 1994.

Chapter 28

1. Fort Dix. New Hanover Township, NJ.

2. The King Cole Trio. "The Christmas Song." Christmas Album. 1960.

3. *Bullit*. Directed by Peter Yates, Solar Productions, 1968.

MAMA RUSSO'S PIZZERIA

Where Our Main Ingredient is Family.

215-660-9602

608 Philadelphia Ave Trevose, PA 19053 • mamarussospizzeria.com

Made in the USA
Monee, IL
04 May 2025